Kingdom Education

GOD'S PLAN
FOR EDUCATING
FUTURE GENERATIONS

Glen Schultz

WITH A FOREWORD BY JOSH MCDOWELL

ISBN 978-0-6330-9-1309
Item 001196830

Dewey decimal classification: 371.07
Subject heading: CHURCH EDUCATION

To order additional copies of this resource: write LifeWay Church Resources Customer
Service; One LifeWay Plaza; Nashville TN 37234-0113; fax order to (615) 251-5933;
phone toll free (800) 458-2772; order online at *www.lifeway.com;*
e-mail *orderentry@lifeway.com;* or visit the LifeWay Christian Store serving you.

Printed in the United States of America

Leadership and Adult Publishing
One LifeWay Plaza
Nashville, TN 37234-0175

DEDICATION

This book is dedicated to families everywhere who want God's best for their children. It has been my purpose to provide encouragement to them through the things God has taught me about educating children.

Specifically, I dedicate this book to the one who has been my partner in providing kingdom education for my children—my wonderful wife, Sharon. And finally, I dedicate this book to my three children, Michael, Teri, and Jason, whose walks with the Lord are my greatest joy in life.

CONTENTS

FOREWORD

As I minister to hundreds of thousands of Christian teenagers and parents around the world, I am increasingly disturbed over several realities seen in the Christian church. These are

- The continual disintegration of the family
- The weakening of the impact of the church on the culture
- The growing number of teens leaving the church

Parents are struggling with knowing how they are to build strong families and raise godly children in a postmodern world. Church leaders are frustrated because they cannot significantly impact their members because of the small amount of time the average member attends church. At the same time the world has access to Christians 24 hours of every day of the week. The results are that society is becoming more and more secular and Christians are embracing this man-centered, secular popular culture.

If the home and church do not turn back to and obey the truths of God's Word concerning how children and youth are to be raised, the influence of Christianity on society will continue its decline. This is why I believe that the principles set forth in this book are critical to reversing these current trends in the church.

Church leaders need to study these pages and evaluate their current programs, teach and train every parent about these principles, and consider how their churches need to expand their ministries in order to support the family in providing biblically based education throughout the week. Christian parents need to know and commit themselves to consistently practice these principles in every aspect of their efforts to raise their children—especially in education. Christian educators must understand and implement these principles to ensure that Christian schools, colleges, universities and seminaries are operating from a biblical philosophy of education that will develop a biblical worldview in every student's heart and mind.

It has been a long slow drift to bring us to this current condition. It will take a long sustained effort to turn the ship around. My concern over this crisis in Christianity has led me to release a new resource, *Beyond Beliefs to Convictions*, and to launch a new campaign to help the family and the church raise a godly generation in Christ. *Kingdom Education* must be an essential element in this effort if the church and the home are going to be successful in this task.

> *The ideal way to help our kids not only to reject the postmodern worldview but also embrace deepened Christian convictions is to align church, home, and school into a unified whole that arms our children with the truth and protects them from distortions.*[1]

Kingdom Education provides Christians with the game plan that can make this alignment a reality.

JOSH MCDOWELL

ACKNOWLEDGEMENTS

I want to thank several people without whose help this book would have remained mere ideas in my mind. First, I want to thank Norma J. Goldman, whose editorial leadership helped hone my thoughts into crisp, clear words that brought meaning to every chapter of this book.

A special word of thanks is due several important people. One is Linda Grammer, whose tireless efforts to take the first rough manuscript and turn it into a finished product is greatly appreciated. The work of Helen Owens, Linda Bond, and Jim Campbell was critical to making this second edition a reality.

Then, there were those special individuals who helped with the production of this book. Pat Brown led the product ideation team in keeping the project on schedule. Dr. Michael Miller consistently reviewed the rough drafts and provided encouragement and insight that strengthened the book's meaning. Dr. Frank Lewis and Joyce Aylor must also be mentioned for providing valuable assistance by doing a final reading of the manuscript prior to going to press.

Finally, a big thank you goes to my entire section staff and my family who kept everything else in life moving forward while I devoted my time to this project.

INTRODUCTION: THE IMPORTANCE OF EDUCATION

What will our society be like in 20 years? What will our homes be like in this same period of time? What type of person will be sitting in our church pews each Sunday in the next decade? These were a few of the questions that weighed heavily on my heart and mind just a few short years ago as I began writing *Kingdom Education*. I was fearful of what society, the family and the church were going to face over the next 10 to 20 years.

Since *Kingdom Education* was first released, I have witnessed an alarming increase in the secularization of not only the culture but also of Christianity. When I first wrote this book, Pollster George Barna had found that only 7 to 8 percent of those identifying themselves as Christians then were biblical in their understanding. He believed that our society was headed for spiritual revival or moral anarchy and that the generation that would determine which direction we would take was sitting in classrooms at the time.[1] Therefore, these vital questions demanded answers if the body of Christ would be effective in fulfilling the Great Commission. Barna's predictions underscored my own belief that there was nothing more important to the future of the home, the church, and society than the proper education of our children and youth.

I never imagined how fast our country would begin living out the secular humanistic philosophies that have dominated American education for the past 100 plus years. Dr. Ravi Zacharias, in a speech given at Amsterdam 2000, stated that there have been five major changes that have had significant impact on cultures around the world.

1. The willingness of atheism to live with its dire consequences.
2. The sweeping impact of eastern mysticism that will deny the uniqueness of Christ.
3. The controlling impact of the visual.
4. The rising reality of a youth-oriented world.
5. The lost center of cultural molding that has resulted in the loss of a single source of authority with the right to lay claim to moral direction.

Dr. Zacharias challenged his audience with a question that faces Christians today: *"How do you reach a generation that hears with its eyes and thinks with its feelings?"*[2]

Recent studies now claim that only *7 percent of born-again teenagers base moral choices on biblical principles.* Eighty three percent of teens said moral truth depends on the circumstances. These studies found that the most common basis for moral decision-making was doing whatever feels right or comfortable in a situation. "The alarmingly fast decline of moral foundations among our young people has culminated in a one-word worldview: 'whatever.'"[3]

In June 2002, the Ninth Circuit Court of Appeals passed down a ruling that declared the pledge to the flag of the United States was unconstitutional. The basis for their hallmark decision centered on two words contained in the pledge—*under God.* While shock and outrage was expressed from just about every segment of society, this ruling should not come as a surprise to Christians. Shouldn't this be the expected result of decades of educational philosophies based on tolerance, relativism, and subjectivism? Therefore, the message of this book is even more important to the future of Christianity in our country than when it was first released.

Ever since the creation of man, there has been a need to educate people correctly. When God created man, He instructed him to "have dominion over the earth." This meant that he would need to learn much about God's creation in order to fulfill this command. Adam's first assignment was to name all the animals so that future generations would be able to identify all that God had created. From this initial assignment man began the process of passing knowledge (education) from one generation to the next. Throughout successive eras, there has been a continuing emphasis on training children to live a productive life here on earth and to relate individually to God's creative intention.

Today, we find ourselves reeling from more than four decades of moral decline in society. Crime rates are soaring, the family unit is disintegrating, and the church has lost much of its ability to be salt and light to the world. Many experts claim that education is the only hope for tomorrow. However, the education system now in place has removed God and His Word from its classrooms. Therefore, all the efforts to improve the educational programs have only led to further problems and greater frustrations for many parents.

Since it is God who created this world and its inhabitants, it is He, alone, who can tell us how to stem the tide of this moral decline. In the Bible, God gives the home and the church the fundamental principles of how our children should be educated. If we are to make a difference in this world, we must once again follow God's instruction on how the home and church are to train future generations. Responsibility for training children has always belonged in the home, with the church joining forces with the parents since the day of Pentecost.

Although schools are not specifically mentioned in the Bible, they have become a part of the fabric of today's society. Therefore, Christians must determine just how the school is to fit into God's scheme of education. We cannot separate the school from the home or the church and be successful, from God's perspective, when it comes to the education of today's children and youth.

It has taken many years for us to arrive at our present condition. It will take several years for us to return to a proper perspective of education. But if we do not begin immediately, the future of the church around the world will be in danger of becoming less and less effective in its mission to bring people to Christ.

A quick look at history emphasizes the importance of education to the future of our society. Emil Brunner presented a speech to the Presbyterian Synod of Virginia in 1941. His words sound a warning that Christians today must heed.

Ah, there is where you make your mistake. The paganism of Germany was not a sudden thing. For over half a century God and religion have been gradually disappearing from the schools of Germany. Education has become secular. A generation has arisen which acknowledges no God and no longer regards those basic moral sanctions which are the safeguard of national and international harmony and decency. That is why the *churches of Germany are empty* and the *nation has turned its face toward the darkness* in the wake of Adolph Hitler.[4] (emphasis mine)

Kingdom education must be in control in the homes, the churches, and the schools of our society if we are to avoid repeating this tragic scenario.

In the pages that follow, we will outline a biblical philosophy that Christian parents, church leaders, and Christian educators must follow in educating their child(ren). A model for kingdom education could be likened to a milking stool. If there were two or four legs on the stool, it would lose stability when placed on an uneven surface. However, when there are three legs, a stool will provide a stable foundation on which an individual can safely rest, regardless of the roughness of the ground.

When biblical principles of teaching and learning are applied consistently at home, at church, and at school, the child will have a firm foundation laid on which he can live a life pleasing to the Lord. It is essential that all three legs—home, church, and school—follow God's prescription for training children and youth. If any one of the legs of the stool of education is not based on a *biblical* philosophy, the education system will have a greater tendency to fail.

We would be wise to study how the Jewish community has maintained its culture regardless of its geographical location or size of its membership. The reality is that every individual in the community has the same goal for every Jewish baby. That goal is to instill within that child the Jewish faith. Every true Jew, in the home, the synagogue, or the school, operates from the same set of beliefs and values. They all work together to ensure that the young child will grow and remain faithful to their religion.

This pattern was set back in the time of the ancient Hebrews. The Hebrews always carefully protected their children from the teachings of

"Greek wisdom" that were not based on the absolute existence of God. In the Talmud, we are told of a young man who went to his uncle, a rabbi, with a request to study "Greek wisdom." The uncle reminded him of Joshua 1:8 and the command to meditate on God's Word day and night. "'Go then,' said the wise rabbi, 'and find a time that is neither day nor night, and learn Greek wisdom.'"5

Can you see how vital it is that Christian parents, church leaders, and school leaders realize that the whole matter of kingdom education must be a joint endeavor? We must stop the fighting over budgets, space, and programs and keep focused on God's command to do all we can to make disciples, "teaching them to observe all things that I have commanded" (Matt. 28:20, NKJV).

We must also recognize that the term "school" has come to mean a place more than a process. In this book, "school" will refer to the education of children and youth during the weekday time period. This would include weekday early education, preschool, elementary school, middle school, high school, and home school. Whatever the age group or the type of schooling chosen, the biblical principles remain constant and must drive the educational process.

It is not the intent of this book to convince every church to start a school. It *is* my intent to make every Christian aware of God's plan for training children and youth and then to motivate them to be sure that their children are receiving such an education. If we are successful in this effort, it is my sincere belief that the next generation can be trained in such a way that they can go out and "turn their world upside down for Christ" (see Acts 17:6, KJV). The downward spiral of moral decline can be halted, the family unit can be rebuilt, and the church can once again become salt and light in our culture.

Section I

IN THE BEGINNING

The end then of learning is to repair the ruins of our first parents.[1]
John Milton

If the body of Christ is ever to develop a proper educational system for its children, we must go back and refocus on education as it was when God created this world. There are two fundamental questions that we must answer if we are to be able to discern the mind of God as it relates to education. The first question is this. *Is education necessary?* The second question is of equal importance. *If education is necessary, when did it become so?*

It must be noted that the term "education" is not found in the Bible. However, the Bible has a great deal to say about *teaching, instructing, training,* and *discipling.* Each of these terms is closely related to the term "education." There are many definitions of education, but this one summarizes them well:

> The process by which children and youth develop knowledge, skills, ability and character especially through formal instruction, training and study.[2]

With this definition in mind, the terms *training, instruction,* and *education* are used interchangeably throughout this book.

The answers to both of the questions presented above are found in God's account of His creation of man. In Genesis 1, we find the marvelous account of God's creation of this world. The crowning point of His creation is described in verses 26 through 31. Here we find that God created man after His own image. This special creative act sets man apart from all other forms of life created by God, for only man was created with a body, a soul, and a spirit. One of the most amazing aspects of God's creation of man is that He formed man's mind with the ability to know and to reason. With this wonderful mind man could know his Creator in a personal way.

In verse 28, God's Word states that man was given dominion, or rule, over the rest of God's creation. Man's responsibility to have control over the animals is clearly evidenced in Genesis 2:19-20. God brought every animal before Adam, and Adam gave each one its name. What a wonderful position Adam had when he was first created by God!

Education was much different in the garden of Eden. Adam had a direct personal relationship with God, his Creator. When Adam needed to learn something, he could go to God, and God would teach him about anything in the created world.

For example, in Genesis 2:18 God had already declared that it was not good for man to live alone and that He would make a helper suitable for Adam. As Adam gave names to every creature God had made, he also learned that no suitable helper was found for himself among them. God knew from the beginning that Adam would not find a suitable helper from any created animal. However, God wanted Adam to know this before He made Eve from Adam's side. The exercise of naming the animals was Adam's education by his Creator in preparation for the creation of Eve.

Unfortunately, this perfect condition did not last long. When Satan tempted Eve, both Adam and Eve disobeyed God and ate of the forbidden fruit from the tree of knowledge of good and evil. The result was that sin entered the world, and Adam experienced separation from God for the first time. From that dreadful point of human history until the future return of Christ to the earth, every person has been born with a sinful nature and is in need of regeneration by God's Spirit.

Something else very significant took place that day in the garden. Satan used a technique with Eve that he still uses in the world today to lead people away from God. In Genesis 3:5, Satan told Eve, "For God knows that when you eat of it your eyes will be opened, and you will be *like* God, *knowing* good and evil" (NIV, emphasis mine). Eve was led to believe that if she were to eat of this tree, she would know everything and be all wise.

The devastation caused by this one disobedient act has affected every person who has ever lived. Man's mind became blinded, and he lost the ability to know God and, therefore, to know good. Instead of becoming like God, man discovered evil. Every parent learns very quickly that a child automatically knows how to do those things that are wrong. The difficult part is teaching him what is right and getting him to do those things. From this account, it is plain to see that education is still necessary. However its purpose changed at the moment when sin entered the world. Since sin is still bound in the heart of every child, education is now necessary in order for him to know right from wrong.

Only through proper instruction and training would future generations come to realize their sinful nature and their need of a savior. Every child born into this world needs proper training in order to know right from wrong. Thus man has always needed education. However, the danger of many educational efforts throughout history is still the same one that Eve faced on that dreadful day when deceived by Satan—the belief that education can improve a person and society.

A *New York Times Magazine* poll, "The Way We Live Now," reports that 73 percent of adults believe all people are born inherently good.[3] When an individual or a society believes that people are born good, it means that man can be perfected by providing everyone with two basic things—a good education and a good environment. Just as Satan deceived Eve by telling her that she would know everything (just like God) if she would only eat of the tree of knowledge of good and evil, he continues to deceive us by telling us that eating of the tree of education will make us perfect.

For example, we have a teenage pregnancy crisis and a rise in use of drugs and alcohol by our children. Society's cure to these problems is education—in the form of sex and drug education. If we could have more and better education programs like these, society says we would solve all of these problems and God would no longer be necessary.

Too often man approaches education as a means of perfecting himself and, in essence, making himself his own god. Christians must never forget that education in any form can never perfect one single individual. Only salvation in Christ can perfect a person.

Christians cannot afford to fall prey to such philosophies when dealing with the education of their children. We must always remember that education, no matter how good it is, can never transform a life. It can never produce a moral person or a moral society. Only the redemptive work of Christ can perform such a miracle.

What then is the true purpose of education for a Christian? What does the term "kingdom education" really mean? What roles do the home, the church, and the school play in the educational process? These are just a few of the questions that I will discuss in this book. Having been a teacher, a coach, a high school principal, and a school superintendent, I have learned much about educational programs and institutions. Having been an associate pastor of a church, I have been involved in many of the educational efforts taking place in the church. And, of course, raising three children has given me insight into what it is like to attempt to train children in the home.

However, the greatest impact on my life has been the influence of God's Spirit leading me into an understanding of the principles found in God's Word concerning the education of children and youth. My education is far from complete, but with each additional day that I am personally involved in education, God teaches me more and more about what He desires for future generations.

As I have poured over the Scriptures and God has revealed His truth to me concerning how Christians are to educate children, I have discovered nine biblical principles to guide us each step of the way. These principles are at the very foundation of kingdom education.

1. *The education of children and youth is the primary responsibility of parents.*
Deuteronomy 6:4-9; 11:18-21; Psalm 78;1-7; 127:3;
Proverbs 22:6; Malachi 2:13-16; Ephesians 6:4

2. *The education of children and youth is a 24-hours-a-day, 7-days-a-week process that continues from birth till maturity.*
Deuteronomy 6:7; 11:19; Proverbs 22:6

3. *The education of children and youth must have as its primary goals the salvation of and discipleship of the next generation.*
Psalm 78:6-7; Matthew 28:19-20

4. *The education of children and youth must be based on God's Word as absolute truth.*
Matthew 24:35; Psalm 119

5. *The education of children and youth must hold Christ as preeminent in all of life.*
Colossians 2:3,6-10

6. *The education of children and youth must not hinder the spiritual and moral development of the next generation.*
Matthew 18:6; 19:13-14; Mark 10:13-16; Luke 18:15-17

7. *The education of children and youth, if and when delegated to others by parents, must be done by teachers chosen with utmost care to ensure that they all follow these principles.*

Exodus 18:21; I Samuel 1:27-28; 3:1-10

8. *The education of children and youth results in the formation of a belief system or worldview that will be patterned after the belief systems or worldviews of the person's teachers.*

Luke 6:40

9. *The education of children and youth must lead to true wisdom by connecting all knowledge to a biblical worldview frame of reference.*

Romans 1:20; Psalm 19:1; 104:24; 136:5; Proverbs 4:5,7; 3:19; 9:10;
Jeremiah 10:12; Romans 11:33; Luke 11:52;
Colossians 2:3; 1 Corinthians 8:1: 13:8; Romans 1:28

10. *The education of children and youth must have a view of the future that includes the eternal perspective.*

Colossians 3:1-2; 3:23-24; Matthew 6:19-20; 2 Timothy 4:6-8;
Acts 20:24; Hebrews 11:13; Colossians

Consider carefully each of these principles. Read the Scripture related to each principle and then ask God to lead you to a deeper understanding as you continue in your study of *Kingdom Education: God's Plan For Educating Future Generations.* (For a complete study of these principles, see the Appendix.)

God created man to have fellowship with Him. Sin broke this fellowship, but it is restored when an individual accepts Jesus Christ as personal Savior. John 17:3 states "Now this is eternal life: that they may know you, the only true God, and Jesus Christ, whom you have sent" (NIV). Salvation opens the mind of an individual to knowing God and learning of God's special purpose for him in life. With our new life in Christ, our minds are able to learn truth and enter into an intimate relationship with Him. As we take full advantage of this ability to know and experience God, we must make this our focus when discussing the education of future generations.

It is time that Christians give full attention to what God has to say about the training of children and youth. The future of the body of Christ will be influenced by how we educate future generations. We can no longer keep the status quo. We must do everything we can to make sure that we are providing our children with a consistent educational process that is true to God's Word. Many of the concepts that you will read about throughout this book may challenge your current thoughts and ideas concerning education. However, I urge you to ask God to reveal to you His principles of true education.

The first section of this book will present a definition and a model for kingdom education. These tools will help us see how we must provide a consistent educational process for our children at home, at church, and at school. As we discuss the real purpose behind education, we will see what results can and cannot be guaranteed from education. We will study together the importance of such things as the development of a biblical worldview, the proper focus of our training, and what factors determine educational outcomes.

In subsequent sections we will look into God's Word to see whom God holds accountable for the proper training of children and youth. We will see the roles that the home, the church, and the school are to play in the educational process, and our discussion will lead us to examine how each of these institutions relates to education and to each other.

Finally, I will present a challenge to every Christian adult. This challenge will include a plan of action that I believe every Christian parent, church leader, and Christian school educator needs to undertaken. I believe that if we carefully study God's Word, follow His instruction, and act decisively, we can train the next generation through kingdom education in such an effective way that our children can go out and change their world for Christ.

As we begin this journey together, I pray that each reader will open his heart and mind to the leading of the Holy Spirit. May each of us ask Him to guide us into truth. Then I pray we will have the faith to trust God completely and act upon what He tells us to do. Only then can our children be educated in a way that will cause them to put their hope in God and to keep His commandments.

2

DEFINING KINGDOM EDUCATION

The Christian school is the only system, outside the home,
where the teachers will instill in your child a biblical worldview.[1]
Glen Schultz

The term "kingdom education" is rarely used in Christian circles today. The term "Christian education" is much more prevalent. However, Christian education has become narrowly defined by various groups within the body of Christ. Some believe it only refers to what happens in a Sunday School setting, others believe it deals specifically with Christian schooling, while still others define it as Christian higher education.

Because of this fragmented concept of Christian education, I want us to think about a unique phrase, *kingdom education.* The kingdom of God is an extremely important concept to every believer. We often hear about how the "kingdom of God" is growing. We are admonished by our pastors to be busy doing "kingdom work." Books have been written on the subjects of kingdom principles for church growth and kingdom leadership. But what do we really mean by these "kingdom" references?

Dr. Gene Mims in his book, *Thine Is The Kingdom,* gives us a clear definition for God's kingdom: "the kingdom of God is the reign of God through Jesus Christ in the lives of persons as evidenced by God's activity in, through, and around them."[2] This definition makes it clear that God's kingdom is a present reality. It is not a physical kingdom but a spiritual one. This spiritual reality should impact the total life of every Christian.

You and I must constantly remember that God is at work in His kingdom right now. As we see Him work, He invites us to be a part of His plans

---

and purposes for mankind. This concept has been wonderfully captured in Henry Blackaby's work, *Experiencing God: Knowing and Doing the Will of God*,[3] a book for every believer's library.

Most Christians readily agree that what takes place in the home and the church should be guided by God's kingdom principles. However, God's principles concerning the education of our children outside the home and church have been overlooked, misunderstood, and, in some cases, totally rejected by the majority of Christians for too long a time.

God's Word warns us about ignoring God's reign in all of life in Paul's letter to the Colossians.

> *Be careful that no one takes you captive through philosophies and empty deceit based on human tradition, based on the elemental forces of the world, and not based on Christ (Col. 2:8, HCSB).*

This is exactly what the scribes and the Pharisees were guilty of in Jesus' days on earth. When they challenged Him concerning some of the practices of His disciples, Jesus responded by exposing the dangers of false teaching (education).

> *Why do you break God's commandments because of your tradition? (Matt. 15:3, HCSB).*

These men were teaching children how to treat their parents. However, their teaching followed their traditions and not God's Word. Jesus condemned them with these words.

> *In this way you have revoked God's word because of your tradition. Hypocrites! Isaiah prophesied correctly about you when he said:*
> *This people honor Me with their lips,*
> *but their heart is far from Me.*
> *They worship Me in vain,*
> *teaching as doctrines the commands of men.*
> *(Matt. 15:6-9, HCSB).*

The same situation is occurring in Christianity today. There are few areas of life that are based solely on human tradition more than the area of education. If we are honest with ourselves, we would have to admit that our current educational processes are based on human traditions and the elemental forces of the world rather than on Christ.

Failure to understand kingdom education has lead to some devastating results in the vitality of both the Christian home and church today. Consider this statement by President Bell of Saint Stephens College.

> We are sending forth graduates with diffused minds, scarcely fit to take command of their own lives or to cooperate in the development of a social state; drifters into conformity and essential human futility; easy victims to specious crowd psychologies; followers of what seem easy ways out. ... They esteem themselves only creatures of their environment and so they tend to become just that. They have little or no perception of standards—of truth, beauty, or goodness; they have no goals of purposeful perfection with which to estimate values or by which to gauge achievement. All things are to them relative—relative not to absolutes but to expediency. Truth means to them little more than a body of observable facts; beauty, conformity to fashion; goodness, doing the things that will make one comfortable or popular. Out of our most able youth, capable of high adventure, we are manufacturing mental and ethical jellyfish.[4]

When most Christians read this quote, they agree that it points out some very troubling traits of today's youth. Through the teaching of evolutionary and existential philosophies, our youth allow expediency, popularity, and relative values to direct their lives.

When I read Bell's quote, I found myself broken over the condition of the youth he described. However, my greatest dismay was not over the words he spoke, but over the year in which he spoke them. For Bell did not pen these words in recent days; he did so in the year *1927!* Bell spoke prophetically, but few paid any attention.

Today, the youth of our country are referred to as "generation Xer's." This generation of youth is one of seekers. They are on a desperate search for meaning and purpose in life. The climate for this search has not developed overnight. It has happened over several decades of cultural shifts in our society. An unknown author captured this downward societal slide when he wrote the following:

In the 1950s, kids lost their INNOCENCE
They were liberated from their parents by well-paying jobs, cars and lyrics in music that gave rise to a new term—the *generation gap.*

In the 1960s, kids lost their AUTHORITY
It was the decade of protest—church, state, parents were all called into question and found wanting. Their authority was rejected, yet nothing ever replaced it.

In the 1970s, kids lost their LOVE
It was the decade of me-ism, dominated by hyphenated words beginning with self: self-image, self-esteem, self-assertion. It made for a lonely world. Kids learned everything there was to know about sex but forgot everything there was to know about love, and no one had the nerve to tell them there was a difference.

In the 1980s, kids lost their HOPE
Stripped of innocence, authority, and love, and plagued by the horror of a nuclear nightmare, large and growing numbers of this generation stopped believing in the future.[5]

When this book was first published, we were only two years from the end of another decade—the 1990s. I thought that the 90s would not be another decade marked by a significant loss of purpose in the lives of our kids. Today, having reflected on the 90s, I have to acknowledge that our kids did suffer great losses during those years, so I have written the following:

In the 1990s, kids lost the MEANING OF TRUTH
It was the decade when our national leaders redefined truth to be merely that which was *legally accurate.* Public opinion polls defined moral truth while the church sat by quietly and watched.

A change in the meaning of truth occurred over a long period of time. It took place through a slow deliberate process driven primarily by educational philosophies. At one time, truth was believed to be *absolute* and *objective.* Some things were believed true for all times, all circumstances, and all people. The purpose of education was to teach students to *discover* truth so that they would know how to live moral lives.

The influence of Enlightenment philosophy changed truth from being absolute to something that is always *relative*. The purpose of education also changed. It became a process by which students would learn how to *adapt* truth to fit different circumstances.

In 1972, Simon, Howe and Kerschenbaum released an extremely influential book, *Values Clarification*. The purpose of this book was clearly spelled out on its back cover.

> Designed to engage students and teachers in the active formulation and examination of values … it does not teach a particular set of values. There is no sermonizing or moralizing. The goal is to involve students in practical experiences [i.e. *lifeboat games*], making them aware of *their own* feelings, *their own* ideas, *their own* beliefs, so that choices and decisions they make are conscious and deliberate, based on *their own* value systems (emphasis mine).[6]

Sidney Simon, one of the main architects of this theory of education, commented on his teaching of high school students. "I always bootlegged the values stuff. I was assigned to teach social studies in elementary school and I taught values clarification. I was assigned current trends in American education and I taught my trend."[7] He went on to say, "Keep it subtle, keep it quiet, or the parents will really get upset."[8]

This concept of relative truth found its way into many textbooks in our schools. One sociology textbook states:

> There are exceptions to almost all moral laws, depending on the situation. What is wrong in one instance may be right in another. Most children learn that is wrong to lie. But later they may learn that it is tactless, if not actually wrong, not to lie under certain circumstances.[9]

Today's culture is under the influence of postmodern philosophy. Postmodernism states that there is no such thing as truth. Therefore, education serves the purpose of guiding students to create truth that is in accord with their individual belief systems. Truth becomes a social construct of a given culture; ideas must be formulated using the language of that culture. Richard Rorty, humanities professor at the University of Virginia, argues that truth that transcends culture is not possible. This is because "where there are no sentences there is no truth, and sentences and their respective languages are human creations."[10]

Since all truth is created by individuals, then all truth must be equally valid. Therefore, postmodern thought tells us that there is no truth, only truths. There are no principles, only preferences. This concept is clearly set forth in an article presented by the Josephson Institute of Ethics:

> But while we must insist on honesty and integrity over hypocrisy and corruption, we cannot also claim that a particular religion, political philosophy or sexual orientation is *universally* superior to another. Indeed, allowing the widest possible latitude in matters of personal choice and conscience is critical to upholding the core ethical value of treating all with respect.[11]

This loss of the meaning of truth has had a significant impact on the church. Os Guinness states "we are people with a true, sometimes a deep, experience of God. But we are no longer people of truth."[12]

Loss of the meaning of truth may be the most devastating loss our kids have experienced. I am optimistic and firmly convinced that our children can reclaim that meaning in life. However, this will not be accomplished until Christians know, understand, and commit themselves to the principles of kingdom education.

In trying to develop a definition and a model to explain kingdom education, I searched God's Word rigorously. Many of God's thoughts on this subject became clear from passages in Deuteronomy, Psalms, Proverbs, the Gospels, and Ephesians. I was amazed at how much emphasis on educating future generations God placed in His Word.

Deuteronomy 6 and Psalm 78 were of particular interest to me. These two passages provide us with wonderful insight into God's mind concerning education. In Deuteronomy, we find God instructing His people, preparing them to enter the promised land. Chapter 6 provides us with some of God's first instructions to His children for a long and fruitful life in His kingdom.

In this chapter, God tells the nation of Israel that they need to focus on two things if they are going to find true success. They must first focus on God Himself: "The Lord our God is one Lord: And thou shalt love the

Lord thy God with all thine heart, and with all thy soul, and with all thy might" (Deut. 6:4-5, KJV). This is so important for believers today. We must get back to a singular focus on God that requires us to love Him with all of our being.

Second, He instructed them to focus on the next generation.

> *Thou shalt teach them diligently unto thy children, and shalt talk of them when thou sittest in thine house, and when thou walkest by the way, and when thou liest down, and when thou risest up. And thou shalt bind them for a sign upon thine hand, and they shall be as frontlets between thine eyes. And thou shalt write them upon the posts of thy house, and on thy gates (Deut. 6:7-9, KJV).*

This teaching is reinforced in the first seven verses of Psalm 78.

There can be no doubt that God cares how our children are educated. He makes it abundantly clear that the two most important things in life for an adult are to love God with his or her whole heart and to teach his children to do the same. Once a person enjoys a love relationship with the Lord, he needs to focus on instilling this love in the hearts and minds of the generation to follow.

From these passages of Scripture, I define kingdom education as

> *a life-long, Bible-based, Christ-centered process of*
> *leading a child to Christ,*
> *building a child up in Christ, and*
> *equipping a child to serve Christ!*

In this brief definition are several important implications which present us with fundamentals of true education from God's perspective.

The first implication is that kingdom education is a lifelong process. It is not something that begins Sunday mornings at 9:45 and ends at 11:00. Nor does it begin each weekday morning at 8:00 and end each afternoon at 3:00. Kingdom education begins at birth. It continues 24 hours a day, 7 days a week, 52 weeks a year, and every year that a young person is preparing for adulthood. Even when a person becomes an adult, kingdom education continues so that the child of God can be increasingly conformed to the image of Christ.

The second implication is that the foundation of all truth is the Word of God. Therefore, kingdom education must also be Bible-based. God's Word is inerrant, infallible, and immutable. When education is built upon a biblical foundation, it cannot be shaken by the winds of change that occur within any given society. Consider the words of Spurgeon, Luther, and Swindoll as to the importance of God's Word in education.

> Withdraw from a child the only divine rule of life, and the result will be most lamentable. An education purely secular is the handmaiden of godless skeptics.[13]
>
> *C. H. Spurgeon*

> I advise no one to place his child where the Scriptures do not reign paramount. Every institution that does not unceasingly pursue the study of God's Word becomes corrupt.[14]
>
> *Martin Luther*

> The Bible *IS* the authority, the final resting place of our cares, our worries, our griefs, our tragedies, our sorrows and our surprises. It is the final answer to our *questions, our search.* Turning back to the Scriptures will provide something that nothing else on the entire earth can provide.[15] (emphasis mine)
>
> *Chuck Swindoll*

Finally, this process must be Christ-centered. Colossians 2:3 states that in Christ "are hid all the treasures of wisdom and knowledge" (KJV). All things were created by Christ and for Christ. The reality of the preeminence of Christ must be woven throughout every fiber of true education. Jesus, Himself, gave a strong warning to the educators of His day. He said, "Woe to you experts in the law! You have taken away the *key of knowledge!* You didn't go in yourselves, and you hindered those who were going in" (Luke 11:52, HCSB). Since Christ is the One in whom all wisdom and knowledge are found, He must be preeminent in the total education of our children. If the education we give our children leaves Christ out, they will be hindered from entering into His rest. If this is happening, can we claim to be educating them according to God's plan?

When we study the definition of kingdom education, we can clearly see that this process consists of *two primary actions* and *one primary goal*. Kingdom education is first a process designed to lead a child to Christ. The gospel must be central to all aspects of a child's education. What good would it be if an individual were to become highly educated and never come to know Jesus Christ as his or her personal Savior? Another important point is that kingdom education requires born-again teachers. Only teachers who have experienced God's gift of eternal life can teach children the gospel message.

Second, kingdom education does not stop once a person comes to Christ. Once a child is saved, it is then necessary to build the child up in Christ. Paul referred to this principle in Colossians 2:7 when he wrote that it is important to be "rooted and built up in him, and stablished in the faith" (KJV). Immediately following this verse, Paul warned Christians to beware and not be ruined by philosophies and empty teaching that is based on the traditions of this world and not on the principles of Christ.

In order for a child to be rooted in Christ, we must consider several factors. First, we must recognize that each child is a unique creation of God. Psalm 139 is a marvelous passage of Scripture showing us that each person has been specially designed by the Master Creator, God Himself. This means that every child will have special gifts or talents. True education recognizes these gifts and is designed to develop each talent to the fullest.

As a father of three, I quickly learned how God had designed my two sons and my daughter with unique abilities. One was very analytical by nature. Another was more strong-willed but extremely creative. The third child was gifted with strong relational skills. Each one learned according to a different learning style. Today, learning styles are seen as a very important aspect of effective education. Many excellent resources on this topic are available to teachers and parents to help them in the process of building up our children in Christ.

Finally, we need to give attention to the ultimate goal of kingdom education. Romans 8:29 clearly states that God has predestined every Christian to be conformed to the image of His Son, Jesus Christ. Paul also emphasized the importance of having the right goal when educating others. He wrote "we proclaim Him, warning and teaching everyone with all wisdom, so that we may present everyone mature in Christ" (Col. 1:28, HCSB). As we train our children through kingdom education, they will move toward being more like Christ. Even though we will all eventually be like Christ, it is the goal of kingdom education to equip believers now, enabling them to serve Christ in His kingdom work.

In Dr. Woodrow Kroll's book entitled *The Vanishing Ministry,* he points out the need for more Christians to answer God's call to full-time ministry. Dr. Kroll states that too many of our educational efforts are aimed at helping our youth find careers that will provide them with comfortable lifestyles rather than developing a Christ-like character that can be used by God in evangelizing the world.[16]

THE TENSION OF KINGDOM EDUCATION

There is a necessary tension found in the principles of kingdom education. Some would say that education should focus totally on the eternal perspective of life. Others argue that we are to love God with *all of our minds,* so we must focus on the academics and leave the spiritual part of education to the home and church. It is vital that Christians fully understand this tension and know how to keep it in proper balance.

Every child is born with two purposes for his or her life, and they are given to each one by God. The first purpose is eternal in nature. God desires for every child to know Him personally through that child's acceptance of Christ as his or her personal Savior.

However, God also puts a temporal call on every life. Once a child accepts Christ as Savior, God desires for that child to grow up with a strong mind so that he or she can effectively serve Him here on this earth. This means that there must always be a balance between these two purposes for our children's lives.

Two quotes demonstrate the tension found in kingdom education. Oswald Chambers summed up the eternal call of God on a child's life when he told a group of students: "One student a year who hears God's call would be sufficient for God to have called this [school] into existence. This [school] as an organisation is not worth anything, it is not academic; it is for nothing else but for God to help Himself to lives. Is He going to help Himself to us, or are we taken up with our conception of what we are going to be?"[17] This is quite a challenge for every parent to consider. As we educate our children are we willing to allow God to help Himself to their lives or are we caught up in what we want them to be?

The other aspect of God's call on our children was summed up by Dr. Albert Mohler, president of Southern Theological Seminary. When addressing a large group of Christian educators, he challenged them with these words, "The Christian school must not be education dressed up for church. It must be the church armed for intellectual battle."[18]

Our children must be armed so they can enter this world and take their stand for Christ without fear or trembling. Their minds must be honed sharp as well as their hearts. When we carefully examine this statement, we quickly recognize that kingdom education is greater than any one part of the training process involving our children. It encompasses the whole of one's education. Sometimes a picture or model can make a particular concept become clearer than words alone. Figure 2.1 illustrates how God's plan for educating future generations spans the entire training process of a child, regardless of where this education takes place.

This model shows the preeminent role of Christ as the ultimate foundation of kingdom education. Paul emphasized this point in 1 Corinthians 3:11 when he wrote that no one can build on any foundation other than that of Jesus Christ. The next building block in our model is a Biblical Philosophy of Education (God's Word). The Bible provides us with specific principles that should mold and shape every aspect of kingdom education. It also provides us with the basis of all truth on which every subject taught must rest. True education cannot exist without both of these foundational building blocks—Jesus Christ and God's Word—in place at all times.

Next the model points out the two functions that make up kingdom education. The first function is evangelism, mentioned in our definition as the leading of a child to Christ. Evangelism is the first act necessary to fulfill Christ's Great Commission given to us in Matthew 28:19-20.

The second function is discipleship, the process of building an individual up in Christ. This function is also found in the Great Commission. Jesus told His disciples that they were to make disciples by teaching those that came to Christ to observe everything that Jesus had commanded them.

The first four building blocks of this model are critical, but the next part of the illustration is the main reason behind this book. If God's plan for education is to be fully effective in the lives of our children, these foundational elements must undergird our children's entire educational process. They must be present in the home, the church, and the school.

A Model for Kingdom Education

Kingdom

Parenting	Home School	Sunday School	Discipleship	Pre-K	K-12	Post Secondary

Home　　　　**Church**　　　　**School**

Discipleship

Evangelism

Biblical Philosophy of Education

Jesus Christ

Education

Figure 2.1

If a country's educational system is to set up true standards, provide right goals, and have real purpose, there should be a coherent worldview undergirding all the planning and teaching that takes place. ... Only Christianity offers this truly all-embracing and realistic world picture.[19]

Kingdom principles of education must guide the entire educational process. Our children need a foundation that is unchanging and consistent, regardless of where the training process is taking place. When kingdom education becomes a reality in a child's life, the home, the church, and the school are providing him/her with a firm foundation. (See Figure 2.2.) The results will build real meaning and purpose in each life, and future generations will once again have hope.

Questions to ponder:
1. Is the education of your children following the principles of Christ or the traditions of this world? Relate this to the education they receive at home, at church, and at school.
2. How has postmodern teaching concerning the denial of absolute truth impacted your life and the lives of your children?
3. Discuss with other believers the definition of kingdom education. Is the education of your children based on the truth of God's Word? Is Christ the key of knowledge, the center of the educational process for your children? What is your goal for your children as reflected by how you are educating them?
4. Do your children have a firm, consistent foundation giving them support in the education that they are receiving at home, church and school?

Setting a Firm Foundation Through Christian Education

Figure 2.2

3

THE END RESULT
OF EDUCATION

*We have failed to stand for truth, failed to articulate, defend and advance
an intelligent and coherent Christian world-view.*[1]
Charles Colson

In this chapter we will explore the results that one can achieve through
education. There has been an enormous amount of emphasis on educational outcomes over the last several years. The term "outcome-based
education" has become a household word in most educational circles.
Many applaud this effort while others vehemently oppose it. However, this
debate is not new by any means. Horace Mann, the father of American
public schools, predicted:

> If American taxpayers could provide education for every child
> in America, within a short period of time the effect of the
> public school system would empty all the jails and prisons in
> the country. ... Let the home and church teach faith and
> values, and the school teach facts.[2]

In sharp contrast, in 1644 John Milton wrote

> The end, then, of learning is to repair the ruins of our first
> parents by regaining to know God aright, and out of that
> knowledge to love Him, to imitate Him, to be like Him.[3]

The fact of the matter is that all education is aimed at developing some type of outcome in the lives of children and youth. Milton captured the right outcome at which true education must aim.

Educational outcomes or results have always been important and will continue to drive any educational process. However, it is equally important to know what education can and cannot do in an individual's life. As we said earlier, we must never forget that education alone cannot perfect an individual or a society. Only God can change a life and, therefore, society. Philip May, in his book *Which Way To Educate*, makes some interesting observations concerning educational outcomes.

> Education is not the source of man's salvation that many have believed it to be. For education, however thorough and enlightened, cannot prevent man from breaking the law of God and of his own nature. It cannot force its pupils to choose the right course and reject the wrong one at every stage. Man, in spite of his education, can and often does violate his rights and duties if he so wishes, and he will sooner or later have to bear the consequences; for man is a sinner.[4]

Parents desire to see their children be successful in life. Therefore, they hope that better education can ensure certain results for their children. Unfortunately, some of the results we work so hard at obtaining cannot be guaranteed through education for all children and may not be the most important results on which to put so much attention. These include such things as academic achievement, physical skill development, and fine arts abilities.

Any child can obtain some degree of accomplishment in these areas. However, education cannot guarantee a specific level of accomplishment for each and every child in any one of these areas. Education cannot even guarantee that a child will become a moral person.

If these statements are true, is there *any* guaranteed result for every child from education? I believe there is such a guarantee. When every young person is educated and enters adulthood, he or she will have developed a worldview. Another term for worldview is a philosophy of life. We define worldview as *the underlying belief system held by an individual that determines his/her attitudes and actions in life.*[5] Each of us has such a belief system which is the driving force behind our attitudes and actions in life.

One of the most important issues Christians must address is the need to develop a biblical worldview in our children's hearts and minds.

> Humans cannot thrive without some sense that there is a purpose for their existence. They need "reference points" that place events, other human beings, and the world generally, into a comprehensive framework that shapes their values, especially their moral compass, and guides their beliefs and actions.[6]

Patrick Morley, in his book *The Rest of Your Life*, also stresses the important role of worldview in everyday life.

> Every person operates from a *base* or *life view*. This base may be Christian, humanistic, or syncretistic. Some carefully chisel out their life view; others merely assume the default values of the cultural majority. ... Some Christians, not anchored in the Word, watch in exasperation as the cross currents of trendy thinking guide their most important choices.[7]

Today we hear a lot of talk concerning "outcome based" education. Of course, secular education sees this as a means of helping students form certain values in their lives. These values are usually centered on tolerance, relativism, and subjectivism. Even though Christians must oppose this form of outcome based education, we must still understand that we are to have desired outcomes for our children as we strive to provide them with a quality education. From the definition of kingdom education, the outcomes we should desire from our children's education are

- to know Jesus Christ as Savior,
- to be continually transformed into the image of Christ, and
- to be fully equipped to serve Christ in everyday life.

Education has always been a major factor in shaping the belief systems or worldviews of individuals and societies. Note in Daniel 1:5 how King Nebuchadnezzar of Babylon designed a three-year training program to fit Daniel and Daniel's friends for service in his kingdom. One commentary on this passage explains how the king's plan indicated the "thoroughness in the Babylonian attempts to erase from their minds all memory of former religious commitment."[8]

Throughout the course of human history, individuals and governments have used education to shape the worldview of their societies. In Germany Hitler taught the German children a philosophy of life based on the beliefs of Nazism. The former Soviet Union instilled a communist worldview into children's minds through a heavily regimented educational program. Teachers in that part of the world have told me that they had to complete successfully two courses in atheism and another course in Darwinian evolution in order to teach in the state's school system. This was required so that teachers would develop an atheistic worldview which they, in turn, would instill in the minds of their students.

Now we see this taking place in Cuba. Chuck Colson, in the November 23, 2001, issue of his *BreakPoint* commentaries reported on the all-out effort of Fidel Castro to instill a communist worldview in the mind of every Cuban child. Colson vividly explained: "Castro knows that in order to keep his regime alive, he must pass the torch of communism to the next generation. ... If he fails to teach Cuba's children the communist worldview, his revolution will eventually die out."[9]

Christian parents, church leaders, and educators must understand how important worldview development is in the education of their children. As we make choices about how we are going to educate our children, we must understand that "our choices have consequences but they often don't show up until we are deeply into a wrong way of thinking and living."[10]

The first step we must take is to understand the different worldviews by which an individual may live his or her life. Dr. David Noebel has established the Summit Ministries with the goal of helping young people understand the importance of developing a proper worldview. In his book *Understanding the Times*, Noebel discusses the wide variety of worldviews prevalent in the world today.[11] It is easy to boil everything down to one simple observation: there are basically only two worldviews possible for a person to hold. One's worldview will be *man-centered* or *God-centered*.

The difference between these two worldviews is extremely critical to the future of society. Colson makes it clear how different these worldviews are. "The huge gulf between the Christian and the secular view of man is sometimes underestimated because there are so many people with a Christian veneer. Many of our neighbors and co-workers don't seem so different from us—on the surface. But their worldview is utterly in conflict with Christian values, and their relativism is dominating a culture that was, until recently, at least nominally Christian."[12] He emphasized his point by referring to a 1990 national study of mainline denominational members that found "only 32 percent believed their faith had anything to do with life outside the church."[13]

A God-centered worldview is sometimes referred to as a *Christian* worldview or a *biblical* worldview. However, using the term *God-centered* hits at the heart of the matter better than the terms *Christian* or *biblical*. A God-centered worldview looks at life with God as the Supreme Being. A man-centered worldview means that God is of secondary importance while man is supreme. To better understand the concept of a worldview, one must realize that any worldview has certain basic components:

- A view of the nature of God
- A view of the nature of man
- A view of knowledge
- A view of right and wrong
- A view of the future

It is important that each of us understands the difference a man-centered and a God-centered worldview makes in each of these components.

A VIEW OF THE NATURE OF GOD

Each and every worldview has a concept of the nature of God. There are those that believe God does not exist. Others believe that God is found in everything, including every person. However, a God-centered worldview holds to the biblical belief that there is only one God, that He created this world, and that He is sovereign in all things. Deuteronomy 6:4 illustrates this view when Moses wrote, "The Lord our God is one Lord!" (KJV).

A man-centered worldview holds the belief that man is the ultimate source of responsibility and power. Listen to the words of the humanist Corliss Lamont when he wrote "that in any case the supernatural, usually conceived of in the form of heavenly gods or immortal heavens, does not exist."[14]

A VIEW OF THE NATURE OF MAN

A man-centered worldview holds to the belief that man has evolved to his current position in the chain of life and is born essentially good or, at the worst, neutral. In child psychology classes, I learned John Locke's view that each child is born as a *tabula rasa,* meaning a blank slate. Of course, this leads to the belief that one's environment and/or education determines future success. Lamont stated, "There is neither original sin nor original virtue. But human nature is essentially flexible and educable."[15]

A God-centered worldview acknowledges that Adam was created in innocence. He then fell into sin, and henceforth all men are born with a sinful nature in need of regeneration by God's Spirit. The world says that this concept of the depravity of man leads to child abuse and neglect. A God-centered worldview counteracts this idea by asserting that every child has worth in God's eyes. It holds to the tenet that education is necessary to show each student his need for salvation. The world, however, fails to recognize that the worth of an individual does not rest in his condition at birth but in the fact that God's Son died on the cross for the sins of every person.

A VIEW OF KNOWLEDGE

A man-centered worldview considers knowledge to be a body of facts. So-called education experts tell us that knowledge is always neutral, explaining that it is always wrong to try to attach any meaning to knowledge in its purest form. Knowledge must, according to the man-centered worldview, be void of any religious overtones, elements of faith, or superstition.

This was not always the case. Before the Enlightenment, knowledge always carried with it certain values that could not be separated from the facts themselves. Since God is truth, then we learn to understand God's nature by pursuing knowledge, wisdom, and understanding. This theme is repeated over and over again in the Proverbs. It is reinforced in Romans 1:20 where we find that we can know and understand God's invisible attributes from studying the things that He created.

Since the creation of the world God's invisible qualities—his eternal power and divine nature—have been clearly seen, being understood from what has been made, so that men are without excuse (NIV).

A God-centered worldview declares that truth is a Person—Jesus Christ.

A VIEW OF RIGHT AND WRONG

Society, from a man-centered worldview, shouts at us that there are no moral absolutes. Of course, society is absolute about this fact! Therefore, I assume society would agree that there is only one absolute. Morality is determined by society and needs no absolute standard. Once again, the words of Lamont sum up this concept: "For humanism no human acts are good or bad in or of themselves. Whether an act is good or bad is judged by its consequences for the individual and society."[16]

In sharp contrast, a person with a God-centered worldview knows that God determines the standard for morality. His standard is absolute and never changes. Regardless of the circumstances, what God says is right *is* right and what He declares to be wrong *is* wrong. Unfortunately, many Christians have adopted a man-centered worldview concerning right and wrong. George Barna reported in a 1991 study that 52 percent of those claiming to be Bible-believing, conservative Christians said there is no such thing as absolute truth![17] By 2000 the percentage of Christians who no longer believed in absolute truth rose to 62 percent. Shortly after the terrorist attacks of September 11, 2001, a survey showed it was approaching 80 percent.[18]

A VIEW OF THE FUTURE

Every worldview presents a concept of what the future is. The existentialist believes that the future is now. Once today is past, it has no relevance for tomorrow. Consider the following humanistic statement concerning a man-centered view of the future. "The central concern is always the happiness of man in this existence not in some fanciful never-never land beyond the grave."[19]

The person with a God-centered worldview realizes that the future is much more than this temporal, earthly existence of mankind. Such a view acknowledges that God is an eternal being, with no beginning and no end. This life on earth is mere preparation for real life that is eternal in nature.

One's view of the future is extremely important when it comes to the matter of education. In "The Psychology of the Future," Alvin Toffler declares, "All education springs from some image of the future. If the image of the future, held by society, is inaccurate, its educational system will betray its youth."[20]

This statement is quite true. Our efforts, as parents, to educate our children are based on our desire to prepare them for the future as we see it. Therefore, it is essential that the view of the future that drives our children's education is accurate. That view must include a literal heaven and hell as the only options for where we will spend eternity. If this is not the case, such an educational system will betray its youth as Toffler predicted. My questions to every Christian adult are *What is our society's image of the future?* and *Based on this image, will society's educational system betray our youth?*

Two factors determine what type of outcome students will develop from their educational experiences:

1. what the educational system believes to be ultimate reality, and

2. what the educational system believes to be ultimate truth.

Our concepts of reality and truth determine our values and, thus, determine the outcomes we see in our children.

Dr. Gerald Stiles, a professor of the history of American education, has studied how our educational system has changed in its beliefs on what is real and what is true over the last 200+ years. Figure 3.1 portrays his findings.[21] To understand this chart, you must keep in mind that what one considers to be real and true determines what we value or desire in an educational outcome. In colonial times, God was the essence of reality, and God's Word was the ultimate source of truth. The colonists wanted to see education develop individuals who were strong in the Christian life.

Soon the Bible and reason became equal in value in determining what was true, while science joined God as the essence of reality. Over the years, we have digressed to the point where New Age thinking is now the essence of reality, and experience determines truth. By New Age thinking, I mean the belief that every person becomes his own god. The result of this shift is

History of American Education*
Gerald Stiles, ED.D.

We the People

	Colonial Education (1620-1776) Christianization	Early National Education (1789-1840) Nationalization	Rise of the State School (1840-1918) Americanization	Remaking of Society (1918-1963) Democratization	Post Christian Era (1963-1993) Individualization	New World Order (1993-) Reculturization
REALITY	God Christ	God Christ Science	Science/God	Science God	Science New Age	New Age Science
TRUTH	Bible Reason	Bible/Reason	Reason Bible Individual Desires	Reason Individual Desires Bible	Individual Desires Reason Experience	Experience Individual Desires
VALUE	Christian Life	Christian Life Good Citizen	Good Citizen Christian Life	Good Citizen Moral Life Self-Actualized	Self-Actualization Good Citizen Morality	Political Correctness Immorality

Used by Permission of Dr. Gerald Stiles

Figure 3.1

xz

that there is an effort to achieve political correctness and immorality (the world calls it amorality) as the most important outcomes from education.

The problem that many Christians have today is that they want education to be like it was in the 1950s and 1960s. Christians remember the general morality that was still prevalent in most schools across our land. However, this is not adequate. Why?

Listen to what Charles Colson says about truth and reality. "Jesus does not claim to be just one truth or one reality among many, but to be ultimate reality—the root of what is and what was—the point of origin and framework for all that we can see and know and understand."[22] He concludes: "All meaning and understanding are rooted in the ultimate reality of God who is. Apart from Him, nothing was created. Apart from Him, we are unable to perceive or to deduce truth about anything."[23] If we do not base our educational efforts on the reality of God, then there is no truth. If there is no truth, "then intellectual pursuits and education become merely a process. Fads displace learning, the intellect withers, and we end up refining the analytical without knowing what is to be analyzed. … With no objective standard to point to what is true or real, music echoes discord; art reflects nothingness; literature stutters into chaos."[24]

Therefore, kingdom education requires us to go back to the time when God was the ultimate source of reality and the Bible was the ultimate source of truth. Only then can we begin to educate our children according to God's plan.

Once we understand the basic components of each and every worldview and how one's concepts of reality and truth determine educational outcomes, we must give careful attention to the proper focus of teaching that is necessary for kingdom education to become a reality. Every Christian must understand these three statements:

- A person's concept of *reality* and *truth* determines his *beliefs!*
- A person's *beliefs* shape his *values!*
- A person's *values* drive his *actions!*

The Making of an Individual

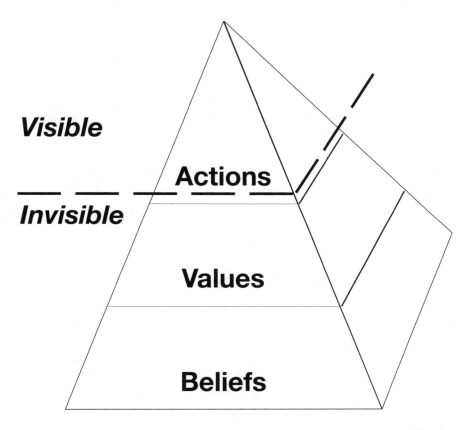

Visible

Actions

Invisible

Values

Beliefs

Figure 3.2

Kingdom education is based on the fact that God is the essence of reality and His Word is ultimate, absolute truth. Its focus is to teach children, youth, and adults that one's beliefs must be determined by these concepts of reality and truth. This is important because our beliefs will eventually determine our actions.

Figure 3.2 illustrates the beliefs, values, and actions of an individual. At the foundation of a person's life, we find his beliefs. These beliefs shape his values, and his values drive his actions. When we observe an individual, we can only see the visible actions of that person. We cannot know what his or her beliefs or values are from a brief glimpse at the person.

How one looks on Sunday when attending church, for example, is not a very good indication of the person's real beliefs and values. Gaebelein noted that "the life of a man reflects his inner beliefs—not those to which he gives outward reverence but those which actually dominate his actions."[25] Morley puts it this way: "The base we build determines the life we live. Only a Christian base will produce a Christian life.[26] "Everyone's life makes a statement about what is important to him."[27]

Too often, Christians have focused their teaching of young people on outward actions or appearances. We are quick to tell our children how to dress, how to act, where to go and not go, what to listen to and watch. Yet, we regularly fail to instruct them in a way that impacts their beliefs.

We must understand that our beliefs matter in life because

- what we believe determines our behavior,
- what we believe counts forever,
- what we believe determines how we serve Christ.[28]

The world has done just the opposite. It stopped emphasizing such things as external appearance and attempted to influence young people internally, through their beliefs. This can be illustrated with the teaching of evolution as science's explanation of the origin of life. This false theory has permeated most of our classrooms across America for the past three to four decades. The emphasis has been on explaining to children that man has evolved to the top of the evolutionary chain of animal life.

This theory goes on to teach its students that man is as much a natural phenomenon as a blade of grass or a weed growing in the yard. If you do not want weeds in your lawn, then the simple solution is to pull them up and throw them away or spray them with weed killer. There is no problem in doing this since it is just a natural part of the survival of the fittest.

To see how this type of teaching has influenced today's youth, we have only to pick up the local paper and read about how human life has been devalued. We should not be shocked to hear about a teenage girl who excuses herself from her date at the prom and proceeds to give birth to a baby. After giving birth, the young lady merely tosses the infant in the trash, allowing the child to die, and returns to the prom as if nothing ever happened. After all, isn't that baby just a mass of tissue that can be discarded (like the weed) if the individual does not believe it is important?

We can add the examples of the decisions made by Timothy McVeigh, Eric Harris, Dylan Klebold, and, even, Mohammed Atta.

This problem is magnified to an even greater extent when we take into consideration the growing crisis of abortion in our society—the ultimate devaluing of human life. The problem we face is bigger than the senseless ending of innocent lives. The Christian's response has been to teach about the evils of murdering the innocent—teaching which we must do. However, by teaching against this evil, we fail to realize that we are once again focusing our teaching on actions.

We must begin teaching to impact our children's *beliefs* according to the nature of God and His Word to the same degree that the world has according to its false philosophies. Josh McDowell makes this point crystal clear when he says, "While we need to fear what our kids could be tempted to do, we need to be more concerned with what our kids are led to believe."[29] When we help our children set biblical beliefs for their lives, they will become people of integrity. True integrity is a "one-to-one correlation between my Bible, my beliefs, and my actions."[30]

In summary, we must understand that the education of a child *will determine* his worldview, and that these principles mandate our full attention. First, we must remember that all education strives to achieve some type of result or outcome for young people. Second, we need to recognize that education cannot guarantee certain academic, physical, or fine arts achievements. It cannot even guarantee the development of a moral individual or society. We must face the reality that every person will leave his or her education and enter adulthood with a worldview. This worldview will be either man-centered or God-centered. *Kingdom education is God's plan to educate future generations to develop a God-centered worldview and, therefore, to think and act according to God's ways.*

4

THE INFLUENCES OF A TEACHER

A teacher impacts eternity; one never knows when his influence will end.
Source Unknown

Kingdom education cannot take place without teachers. Christian adults play a very important role in God's plan for educating future generations. Luke 6:40 states that when a child is fully trained, he will be just like his teacher(s). The most important factor in the development of a young person's worldview is the influence of his teachers. In subsequent chapters, we will discuss God's priority as to who are the most influential people in teaching young people. This chapter will deal with the three main influences all teachers have on those whom they teach.

Having been in the classroom for many years, I have collected a series of sayings that relate to teaching. Think about the following quips and quotes.

- To teach is to touch a life forever!
- You can never erase the influence of a teacher!
- A teacher: preserves the past; reveals the present; creates the future!
- A truly special teacher is very wise; she sees tomorrow in every child's eyes!

When I left my tenure at Lynchburg Christian Academy, one of my students gave me a framed Scripture verse that still hangs on my wall. It reads: "He was ... a mighty teacher, highly regarded by both God and man." This verse from Luke 24:19 is a constant reminder to me of the important

---

role I played as a teacher of young people. Frank Gaebelein once wrote: "The fact is inescapable: The worldview of the teacher, insofar as he is effective, gradually conditions the worldview of the pupil. No man teaches out of a philosophical vacuum. In one way or another, every teacher expresses the convictions he lives by, whether they be spiritually positive or negative."[1]

All teachers exert three major influences that over their students. It is vitally important that we are aware of them as we attempt to follow God's plan of kingdom education. Figure 4.1 presents us with a model of a teacher showing different influences on those being taught.

This diagram shows three concentric circles. Each circle represents a different influence exerted by every teacher. If we start at the center, we see the influence of *content*. This is the influence that is determined by *what I say!* Since we will be influencing future generations by our content, we

The Influences of a Teacher

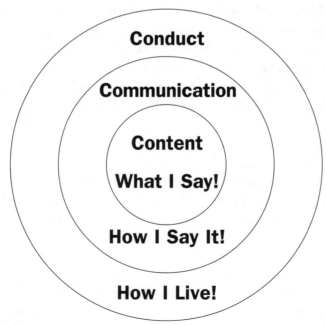

Figure 4.1

must be extremely careful that our children receive truth. It is interesting that James begins chapter 3 of his letter to the saints with the admonition that they not be too quick to be a teacher. He explains that a greater judgment is in store for those who teach. Can you imagine the reaction you would receive if you were to share this verse with teachers you have recruited in a school or a church their very first day on the job?

Why would James make such a bold statement? If we look at the context of this verse, we see that it begins an entire section on the power, both positive and negative, of the tongue. Teachers do a great deal of talking, and they will be held accountable for what they say. Kingdom education requires teachers who will speak the truth. All truth is God's truth and, therefore, God's Word is, and must be, the foundation for teaching. I recently read an article summarizing a speech given by Dr. Albert Mohler, President of Southern Baptist Theological Seminary. The headline of this article read, *"Christian Education Minus Scripture, a 'Lie.' "*[2] God wants teachers in His system who will teach truth.

The second circle in our diagram deals with a teacher's influence of *communication.* This influence comes from *how I say it!* Imagine yourself in a room with a dozen 5-year-old children. They are sitting at little tables and you are their teacher. What do you think would happen if I were to walk into your class, bring my 6'4" frame over little Sandy's chair, fold my arms, look down at her with a stern face, and gruffly say, "Sandy, never forget that God loves you and so do I"? She would probably burst into tears. But why? I told her truth. The problem would not be what I said but *how* I said it. It would have been far more effective had I knelt down at her place, and softly said, "Don't ever forget the wonderful truth that God loves you and so do I."

How we say things sometimes has greater influence than what we say. God's Word gives us instruction about this influence when it declares that we should always speak the truth in love and that our speech should be seasoned with grace. What we say and how we say things are two major influences of every teacher on the lives of others.

The outer circle in our diagram is also very important. This circle represents a teacher's influence through his *conduct.* This influence is demonstrated by *how I live.* We have heard the saying many times, which goes something like this, "Your actions speak louder than words" or "I can't hear a word you are saying, because your actions are speaking so loudly." Personal conduct is one of the most powerful influences a teacher can have on another person.

Think about the teachers you have had throughout your life. What do you remember most about them? Is it the words they spoke? Is it how they communicated with you? Or do you simply remember how they lived and acted? I have many fond memories of Mrs. Kramer, my first-grade teacher. She was also my second-grade teacher. Come to think of it, she was my third and fourth-grade teacher! This happened because I had the privilege of attending a one-room schoolhouse for my first four years of schooling.

Mrs. Kramer lived in the house next door to the school and would arrive very early each morning. In the winter, she would have the pot-belly stove all warm and toasty for us to dry our mittens on when we arrived. I don't remember all that Mrs. Kramer told me. But I do remember vividly how she acted. Her conduct had a lasting impression on me. In fact, it was Mrs. Kramer who took me out to the woodshed and taught me, through her actions, that there were two types of wood kept there. There was the wood that she had me carry in to keep the fire going and there was the wood she used to knock the fire out of me!

When there are contradictions between a teacher's conduct and/or communication and his or her content, 95 percent of the time students will reject the content and accept the conduct or communication they observed. God demands that teachers in His system demonstrate godly conduct. He wants future generations to be taught by individuals who walk godly in Christ Jesus.

Paul understood the importance of these three influences that he had as a teacher in God's plan for educating future generations. In Philippians 4:9, Paul gives some very important instructions to his students as he tells them,

> *Those things, which ye have both learned, and received, and heard, and seen in me, do: and the God of peace shall be with you (KJV).*

This serves as a self-evaluation verse for every teacher involved in kingdom education. Paul said with confidence that if his students would do the things he told them, the God of peace would be with them. Paul spoke truth whenever he was teaching, and he communicated truth in the right way. However, the most powerful part of this verse comes from the fact that Paul promised his students that the God of peace would be with them if they would do the things they saw in him. Paul understood the powerful influence of conduct in kingdom education.

There have been times when the God of peace would not have been with those I was teaching if they had followed my conduct. The attitudes that I expressed or actions I performed on those occasions would have brought different results if they were imitated by my students. They probably would have experienced the God of judgment and righteousness rather than the God of peace.

After teachers understand their influence on their students, they must also give careful attention to the thrust of their teaching. There must be a balance among four teaching thrusts:

1. The thrust of truth—What to believe
2. The thrust of proof—Why to believe it
3. The thrust of application—What to do as a result of believing
4. The thrust of implementation—How to live it out[3]

Our goal is to lead our children to a balanced Christian life. That type of life requires that our children "first know what to believe and, then, as a result, how to live."[4]

Kingdom education demands that teachers know the many ways that they will influence young people. It also requires that our children are under teachers who will teach the truth in love, knowing that how they live will have a lasting impact on those they teach. Kingdom education is God's plan for educating future generations. To fulfill this plan, Christian teachers and parents must know the definition of kingdom education, understand the results that come from kingdom education, and exert the proper influences on those they teach.

Section II

KINGDOM EDUCATION:
THE ROLE OF
THE HOME

5

God's Assignment for Parents

Children need to know God's truth
if they are going to have any chance of success in life.[1]
Glen Schultz

The family has been under strong attack for the past several decades. Recent studies indicate that Christian marriages are just as likely to end in divorce as non-Christian ones.[2] "The family is the germ-cell of civilization,"[3] and yet we see it disintegrating before our very eyes. The current condition of Christian marriages and families is having a devastating effect on our children and youth. The reason for such concern is the fact that the home has been, is, and will continue to be the greatest influence on shaping the next generation. The strength of the home will determine the strength of the church in the future.

Dr. John MacArthur provides parents with some very wise counsel on parenting.

> What we desperately need is a return to *biblical* principles of parenting. Christian parents don't need new, shrink-wrapped programs; they need to apply and obey consistently the few simple principles that are clearly set forth for parents in God's Word.[4]

The first thing parents must understand is the importance of parental responsibility in raising children.

It seems as if it happened only yesterday. I was entering my sophomore year of college. I had enrolled in college calculus and was determined to get an A in the class. At that time, I was in a pre-med course of study, planning to go to medical school upon graduation. In order to achieve the goals I had set, all of the science and math courses I took were extremely important to me.

During the first class, I took careful notes and listened attentively to the professor's instruction. At the end of the class period, the professor assigned ten problems for us to do as homework. I carefully completed all ten problems that night in my dorm room. As I entered the class the next time, I was confident that the problems had been done correctly. Dr. Kauffman proceeded to lecture the entire class time and he then assigned ten more problems for homework. However, he neither collected nor reviewed the first homework assignment.

I assumed he had just forgotten to collect the earlier assignment. So I went back to my room and carefully completed the new assignment. To my amazement, this procedure was repeated for the next couple of classes. I soon realized that Dr. Kauffman was not going to collect or grade these homework assignments. Within a week, I stopped doing the homework. I thought there was no sense in wasting my time since the professor was not even reviewing them in class.

About three weeks into the semester, Dr. Kauffman announced our first major test. I started studying immediately. When the time came to take the test, I was very confident that I would do well. After all, I had studied hard and knew the material well. When the test was given to us, I quickly scanned all the problems. Yes, I had studied the right things, and I knew every answer to the questions on the test!

About halfway through the class period, Dr. Kauffman interrupted the test and announced, "Be sure to turn in all your assignments with your test. The assignments will make up 50 percent of your test grade!" An empty feeling hit me hard. I began perspiring, realizing that I had stopped doing my homework two weeks earlier! Soon my mind went blank, and I could no longer recall the information needed to answer the questions accurately. Of course, I failed that test miserably.

However, I learned a very valuable lesson through that experience. The lesson is this: *I am responsible to complete all assignments given to me—even when no one checks my work on a regular basis!* This lesson would prove to be valuable in many different situations in which I later found myself. This was especially true when my wife and I became parents of three children.

God provides parents with wise instruction in Psalm 127:3-5:

> *Behold, children are a heritage from the Lord, The fruit of the womb is a reward. Like arrows in the hand of a warrior, So are the children of one's youth. Happy is the man who has his quiver full of them; They shall not be ashamed, But shall speak with their enemies in the gate (NKJV).*

Since we are dealing with the topic of education in this book, I would like to paraphrase the first portion of this passage. In educational terms, this passage could read, *Behold, children are God's homework assignment to parents.* When I became a parent, God gave me the assignment of raising my children as gifts from the Lord. I was to bring them up in the nurture and admonition of the Lord. My wife Sharon and I shared the responsibility of training or educating our children according to God's plan. From this passage of Scripture, as well as others found throughout God's Word, it is clear that God assigned the training of children to parents. Too many parents fail to realize that their children are given to them as homework assignments from God Himself. Even though God does not come to our homes and check our assignments regularly, someday we will hear God say, *It is time to turn your homework in to Me for a grade.*

Christian leaders have stressed this truth throughout the history of the church. Overman points out that "Hebrew parents viewed children as entrusted to them by God, and received them as such into their households like divine appointments."[5] MacArthur also emphasizes this truth. "God Himself has given the responsibility for raising children to parents—not to schoolteachers, peers, child-care workers, or other people outside the family—and therefore it is wrong for parents to … shift the blame when things go wrong."[6]

The second chapter of Malachi provides us with tremendous insight as to how important this homework assignment is to God. In verse 14, God explains why He is not giving attention to the sacrifices of Judah. He makes it clear that He is distressed over the marriages of the nation of Israel being in shambles. God said that He sanctifies marriage so that parents can produce godly offspring. Sad to say, there are couples who are unable to have children. However, God desires that every couple with children produce godly offspring. Listen to how Bruce Wilkinson, founder of Walk Thru the Bible Ministries, explains this passage:

Marriage is not only for companionship and for fulfilling His creation commands; the Lord's seeking something from your marriage. The Lord God's seeking offspring—children from your marriage. But a certain kind of offspring. God seeks from you godly offspring![7]

Christians today find themselves in a similar situation as the nation of Judah did. We do all of the religious sacrifices that we think Christians should do—go to church, participate in praise and worship, give the tithe and our offerings and listen to sermons—but it seems as if God does not receive these sacrifices with pleasure and actually disregards them. For example, we pray and ask God to heal our land, and yet the moral decline in our country only increases in intensity.

We ask ourselves why God isn't paying attention to our sacrifices and answering our prayers. What was true for Judah is true for us today. Our homes are in shambles. Divorce runs rampant. The result is that very few homes are producing godly offspring. Parents must grasp the reality that this homework assignment is so important to God that He does not receive our religious sacrifices with pleasure when we do not follow His instructions in raising our children.

I have had the opportunity to travel to various republics within the former Soviet Union. The purpose of these trips was to help Soviet teachers understand how biblical morality can build a foundation for society. Through many conversations with these educators, it became quite apparent that they believe the state, and not the parent, is responsible for educating children. Even in our own country, many parents, including many Christian parents, have abdicated their God-given responsibility to others. Sometimes it has been turned over to the church. Other times it has been given to the schools. However, there is no escaping the fact that God has always held parents responsible for properly training their own children.

Larry Burkett emphasizes the foundation of parental teaching in *Financial Parenting:*

As parents we need to teach our children … on a foundation of teaching children God's Word and principles while directing them toward [God] and helping them to develop a relationship with God. Anything that you can talk your kids into, someone else will be able to talk them out of, so we need to concentrate on building our children's foundation. They need to have it ingrained in them both that the Bible is life's instruction manual and that they need to base their lives on its principles and instructions.[8]

Francis Curran was a professor of the history of American education. He researched the phenomenon of turning to others outside the home and church to formally educate one's children. In his research, he discovered

> ... a revolutionary development in the history of education and in the history of Christianity: the surrender by American Protestantism during the past century of the control of popular elementary education to the state. ... Only in the United States has Protestantism relinquished the traditional claim of the Christian church to exercise control over the formal education of its children in the elementary school. ... The Christian churches eventually agreed that the state must have an important place in the direction of popular elementary education.[9]

Of course, parents had to relinquish this responsibility before the church could do so. The results have been both far reaching and tragic.

In the passage of Scripture that we have been considering, children are compared to arrows. Using this analogy, God has provided us with another important insight into the specific assignment of educating our children. I am not an archer, but I have talked with several individuals who use a bow and arrow for hunting purposes. All of them tell me that their success out in the field depends a great deal on the condition of their arrows. Each arrow must possess three qualities if it is to prove useful. It must be straight. It must be balanced. It must be sharp.

First, the arrow must be *straight*. Imagine being in the woods all day, finally coming upon your prey. You reach for an arrow, aim carefully, and let the arrow fly. Unfortunately, the arrow veers off course and goes into the woods. The arrow you had chosen was not straight. Many times a person will refer to an individual as being straight as an arrow. By this he means this individual possesses certain character qualities, such as honesty and integrity. As we train our children, we must be sure that they are made straight through the gospel. Only salvation through the death, burial, and resurrection of Christ can straighten a sin-crooked life.

The second requirement for an arrow to be useful is to be *balanced*. Those colorful feathers on the end of an arrow are not there simply for decoration. Each feather must be properly placed and trimmed so the arrow has perfect balance when in flight. If the arrow is not balanced, it will wobble and miss the mark. So it is with our assignment as parents. We must see to it that our children are balanced by weaving God's Word into every aspect of their lives.

Finally, an arrow must be *razor sharp*. Can you imagine the frustration of having your prey in your sights, releasing the arrow, and when the arrow hits the target, it merely falls to the ground? The problem was that you failed to put a point on its end. Our children will become sharp by learning how to live their lives fully surrendered to God's Holy Spirit so that they can be useful in God's hand when they become adults.

When I completed my assignment of educating my children, I turned them over to God to be used in His kingdom work. This work is referred to as a spiritual battle in many portions of Scripture. Therefore, God expected to receive my arrows already made straight, balanced, and sharpened. Unfortunately, too many Christian parents are giving God arrows that are like those I received for Christmas as a young child—not very straight, not balanced, and with a small rubber suction cup on the end for a point. This type of arrow is of little use to God.

Psalm 78:1-7 shows us to what extent we must go to complete this assignment successfully. It specifically instructs fathers to *show* and *tell* their children the truth about God and His Word. One of the secrets to the strength of the Hebrew family was the "acceptance of the idea that it was a father's duty to take an active role in the instruction of children in the home."[10] Even though it is true that both parents must take part in educating their children, children desperately need their father's involvement.

This passage clearly states that parents must first *show* then *tell* their children about the things of God if the instruction is going to stick. Think back on the three influences a teacher has on a child that were presented in the previous chapter. One's influence of *content* is sometimes negated by the influence of one's *conduct*. MacArthur reminds us "that there was no deficiency whatsoever in the *content* of Solomon's instruction to his son. Yet by way of *example [conduct]*, Solomon failed, and failed miserably."[11]

He goes on to warn us that "it does no good to teach our children sound wisdom and then live a life that contradicts what we are teaching. ... [There] may be no surer way to provoke your children to despise and discard the wisdom of the Lord."[12]

Psalm 78 also shows us the meaning of the diligence required in educating our children. The Psalmist instructs parents that we must do such a thorough job teaching this to our children that they will, in turn, teach their children who will, likewise, teach their children. The end result will be that this future generation "might put their confidence in God and not forget God's works, but keep His commandments" (Ps. 78:7, HCSB).

This teaching can be compared to a relay race. But this relay race is, by far, the most important relay race that will ever take place in anyone's life. I recently watched a relay race take place on a national television station. As I watched, it occurred to me that this is a picture of what biblical parenting is all about.

A Relay Race

Four runners with sleek muscular bodies take their positions around the track. The first runner takes the baton firmly in his hand. He sets himself in the blocks and coils his powerful body into the starting position. His muscles tighten as he prepares for the start.

At the sound of the starter's gun, he explodes out of the blocks, his eyes fixed on his team's next runner. He quickly expends all of his energy in order to get to the next runner as quickly as possible.

As he nears the next runner, his teammate begins to run away from him. The first runner strains to reach the second runner before he gets too far down the track and is disqualified. He stretches and strains to put the baton firmly in the next runner's hand making sure that it is not dropped.

It has been a matter of mere seconds from the start of the race until the baton is passed to the second runner. Exhausted, the first runner stops and watches as his teammate races toward the third member of the team. He anxiously watches as each teammate passes the baton to the next runner. Adrenaline continues to rush through the first runner's body, driven by the pressure of praying that his effort does not end in defeat.

Exhilaration explodes when the final teammate crosses the finish line with the baton firmly in his grasp. The first runner was successful and his teammates also finished the race without dropping the baton. He can now rejoice!

A Spiritual Relay Race

If you have ever witnessed a relay race as I've described, then you have experienced the tension that surrounds such an event. If your team drops the baton, you feel the dejection that comes from knowing that the race is over and there can be no victory. All of this anticipation and energy is expended in watching a race that lasts for less than a minute and will be forgotten as soon as the next race begins.

Every Christian parent is involved in a similar race, but the stakes in this race are far greater than any other relay ever run. This race determines whether or not our children attain a prize that will last for all eternity. As each successive generation enters the race, the effort of the first parent becomes increasingly more important.

The baton in this race is our faith in Christ—not carried in the hand but in the heart. The goal is to pass the baton of faith from the parent's heart to the child's heart. It is critical that every Christian trains and prepares before entering the parenting race, toning spiritual muscles into peak condition.

As the birth of the first child draws closer, parents are set in the starting blocks, readying themselves for the starter's pistol. With their spiritual lives coiled for action, they must explode out of the blocks the moment birth takes place. This is so critical because as soon as a child is delivered, he starts running away from his parents—it's called growing up. Every parent eventually says that the child grew up too fast. You have heard them say, *"It seems like only yesterday that we were bringing him home from the hospital, and now he is going out into life on his own."*

From birth on, the parent must expend all of his energy to accomplish one goal—the passing on of his faith to his child's heart. He must stretch and strain to get the baton firmly in the grasp of his child's heart before the child gets too far down the racetrack of life. Statistics show that the odds of an individual placing his faith in Christ decrease significantly as the child grows older. When we read in Scripture that "a generation arose that knew not God" (1 Cor. 1:21, KJV), we realize that parents must have dropped the baton.

Once the baton has been securely transferred to the next generation, the pressure remains. The parent must pray and cheer his child on as the child assumes the responsibility for getting the baton into the heart of the third generation.

When his child finally passes that baton on and the parent watches his child walk in truth, he then experiences the exhilaration that comes from victory. *He can now rejoice!*

This analogy causes us to examine everything that we are doing in educating our children. Do we understand the importance of the race? Do we understand and are we committed to successfully completing the homework assignments that God has given us?

As we have seen, doing so will take all of a parent's energy and attention. Judges 2:10-14 relates that the nation of Israel began to lose the Promised Land as a result of failing to teach their children to follow God. Burkett says, "One of the key reasons we sometimes lose our children to our culture is that we don't recognize where we are in history and that what our society is teaching is so different from God's Word."[13]

We need parents today like Joshua. In Joshua 24:15, this man of God made a bold statement before the entire nation of Israel. He declared, "As for me and my house, we *will* serve the Lord." Joshua said that his whole household *would* serve the Lord. He did not say that they would *try* to serve the Lord. According to Wilkinson, "'Try' implies that it really doesn't work. So long as I do my part, then I certainly can't be held accountable for my children's actions."[14]

Do you remember the lesson I learned in college calculus? The professor had not checked the homework assignments on a regular basis. Even though he had not collected these assignments for several weeks, he still expected me to complete them daily. So it is with God's assignment to parents. He may not collect homework, but He expects us to be faithful in doing it daily. We cannot know when He will ask us to turn in our homework for His review, but when He does collect it, we may be surprised as to what He will consider to be important. I am not sure that God will be interested in what courses and programs they had in school or what types of jobs our children have. He won't ask how much money they make, or the type of house or car they possess. I believe that God will want to know if they know Him, love Him, and are faithfully serving Him.

Why aren't parents completing their homework assignment to raise godly offspring? Wilkinson answers: "If you dig deep enough, you will always uncover the real reasons why children are not raised as godly offspring. The parent has another god before the Lord. The parent is seeking something that the Lord does not approve, rather than seeking to raise children that are indeed godly."[15]

Let me share with you something that happened to me recently. I had been invited to preach on this topic at a church in Texas which also sponsored a Christian school. Before I spoke on this particular Sunday morning, a mother shared her testimony. What this mother said made such an impact on my life that I asked permission to share some of her testimony with others. She graciously consented to my request.

> Eight years ago my husband and I made the decision to send our children here [to school]. We based our decision on God's Word which says, "Seek ye first the kingdom of God, and his righteousness; and all these things shall be added unto you" (Matt. 6:33, KJV). This is God's promise that if we seek to put Him first in our children's lives that every single thing that our child needs to fulfill God's perfect plan—not our plan, but God's perfect plan—for their lives will be given unto them.

She then recounted a phone conversation she had had at the end of the school year with Mrs. Clausen, the first-grade teacher of one of her seven-year-old twin daughters, Keaton.

> [Mrs. Clausen] was quite distressed because Keaton had scored poorly on her test and [Mrs. Clausen] naturally felt responsible. My response to her was, "Mrs. Clausen, did you teach my child to love the Word of God? Yes. Did you teach her to praise and worship Jesus? Absolutely, you did. Did you love my little girl with the love of the Lord? Always. Then both you and Keaton have had a successful year. I'm not worried about her test scores." I wasn't. I knew that God would make sure that Keaton had everything she needed to fulfill God's perfect plan for her life. … I am so glad that I didn't worry about Keaton's test scores because test scores don't count in heaven.

I'm so glad that I didn't sweat the small stuff. You might argue that with me, but test scores are small stuff in comparison to knowing Christ.

You might be thinking that this is a typical testimony of a parent who is trying to support a Christian school. However, the reason I am compelled to share Lorin's testimony is because of the words that the news commentator, Paul Harvey, has made so famous—*the rest of the story!* Just a few weeks prior to this service little Keaton had been killed in an accident. The conversation between this mother and this teacher took place weeks before this tragic event.

Lorin went on to share:

I am so grateful that in preparation for Keaton's death the Lord placed my children in a school where for many years they have been saturated with the Word of God and His powerful truths. Though academics are important, it is the Word of God that has seen us through our darkest hours.

Never once has Cameron run to her math book for comfort. Never did we open Presley's science book to find words of encouragement. The facts in Bailey's history book didn't sustain us. Not one time have Conner's spelling words lifted our spirits. It is God's Word and His Word alone that has given us comfort, strength, hope, assurance, peace, and joy.

Life is hard. I want my children to have everything they need when facing the storms that tomorrow will bring. Let me assure you that [this school] equips our children well. They receive a good academic education, but with that they also receive what is most important. They receive a great spiritual foundation.

So, when their little world is rocked, when their dreams are shattered, when their lives are all in pieces, they know what to do. They have been taught to pray. They know what to believe. They have learned God's promises, and they know who to run to, for they have been introduced to Jesus.

Lorin is a mother who understands that each of her children is a special homework assignment from God. She also fully comprehends that God can call the assignment in for a grade at any time. That is why she said:

> Like you, I desire my children to have an excellent academic education, but first and foremost I desire, no, I am desperate, for them to know this awesome God. They must know the One who gives strength to the weary, who gives hope to the hopeless, the One who is able to bring forth beauty from ashes, the One who is able to work all things for good, the One who turns weeping to joy. They must know Jesus and know Him well.
>
> I am so grateful that [this] is a school where my children will not only learn multiplication, they will learn about the one that multiplied the loaves and fishes. Not only will they learn division, but they will learn about the One who divided the Red Sea. They'll learn about the world and its creations, but they will also learn about their creator. They'll learn language and the mechanics of words, but they will also learn about the One who is the Word.[16]

Children truly are God's homework assignment to parents. Raising godly children is the goal of this assignment and must be the home's highest priority. How are you doing on the homework assignment that God has given you?

6

THE TRAINING PROCESS

Rules without relationships will breed rebellion.
Anger assassinates relationships.

One of the most familiar passages of Scripture is found in Proverbs 22:6. Probably most Christian parents have looked at this passage as a promise for their children. The verse reads, "Train up a child in the way he should go: and when he is old, he will not depart from it" (KJV). This short verse carries a great deal of meaning with respect to the education of our children. Too often, we take this verse to mean that if we train our children in the way we think they should go, they will eventually turn out that way.

The term "train up" is rich in meaning that may go undetected at first glance. Originally it was used to describe the action of a midwife at the birth of a baby. The midwife would dip her finger in some sort of plum or prune juice. Then she would massage the gums of the baby with her finger. The bittersweet sensation would cause the newborn baby to begin a sucking motion. At this moment, the midwife would place the baby in his mother's arms for her to nurse. It was important to get the baby to begin the sucking motion so that he could receive the nourishment necessary to sustain life.

We have the same responsibility with our children. It is important that we do those things that will cause our children to desire spiritual nourishment. I heard a pastor paraphrase the verse this way, "Dedicate a child to the Lord and create within him the desire to obtain true wisdom, and when he is grown he will walk with the Lord." From the moment that a child comes into this world, parents need to begin massaging his young heart and mind with the things of the Lord. It is never too early to start reading God's Word to your children. If we do not create a thirst for God in our children's early years, it is doubtful that they will have this desire later in life. Overman makes this point when he says, "If parents do not train their children to acknowledge God they will, through default, train them to ignore Him."[1]

The concept of training up a child also indicates that it is a lengthy process. Kingdom education is a life-long process. This verse in Proverbs indicates that the training or educating process continues from birth until the child reaches maturity. Psychologists tell us that the first five years of a child's life are the most important learning times the child will ever experience. This does not mean, however, that our task is over once the child becomes school age. We must continue with a consistent, continual educational process that creates a desire within our child to know God in a personal way throughout his life.

It is interesting to see Christian parents send their young child to a Christian preschool, only to send him into secular education for the next 12 years. After this, they again turn to a Christian college hoping that the child will complete his education and be ready to serve Christ. God's plan for educating our children requires that we provide them with educational experiences rich in biblical truth throughout their developing years. We must present the truth of God's Word to our children in their preteen and teenage years with the same intensity that we did when they were young.

This training process also requires that we teach each child according to how God created him/her. Training up a child "in the way he should go" could best be translated "in their own way." This means that each child is a unique creation of God and will learn according to his natural bents or tendencies present at birth. The learning process must not only be consistent over time, but it must also be consistent with the abilities and talents with which God has endowed each child.

As we educate our children, it is important to keep a proper balance. Instruction must be both preventive and corrective. Proverbs 22:6 and Proverbs 3:12 point out this two-pronged approach to training children. Figure 6.1 illustrates an important aspect of the training process. It deals with the use of corrective measures when raising a child. The diagram shows how the inward control of a child must always be balanced by outward control. The goal of kingdom education is that a person will always be under control and never out of control at any stage of life. Of course, God's plan calls for the Christian to be under the total control of His Spirit throughout life.

This diagram illustrates that at birth a child does not exhibit any inward control. Therefore, parents must exercise complete outward control over the child. But as the child begins to grow and mature, his inward control increases. As the maturing process takes place, the parents must lessen the use of outward control. It would be wonderful if this move toward maturity would be steady and regular over the entire life span of an individual. Unfortunately, all children will make mistakes and exhibit improper inward control at times. When this happens, parents must increase their outward control over the child for a period of time. Figure 6.2 illustrates this situation. It is important that the increase of control is commensurate with the lack of control demonstrated by the child. If we do not evaluate and balance control, we will either overprotect or over-discipline our children. Either extreme will bring harm to the child and delay the maturing process. As we deal with the discipline or correction of our children, we must remember that a loving parent will always correct

Figure 6.1

the one he or she loves. This correction will require corporal punishment when a child is young. A study of Proverbs reveals the need for this type of correction. God says that the parent who spares the rod actually spoils the child. Using this type of correction in the training of our children is ridiculed by the so-called child experts of our day. However, kingdom education is Bible-based, and therefore, we must follow God's Word when it comes to the corrective part of educating our children.

There are two principles to consider throughout the training process. These two principles will protect us from merely punishing or abusing our children and cause us to give them the loving correction they will need in order to be mature in Christ. These two principles are:

1. Rules without relationships always breed rebellion!
2. Anger assassinates relationships!

I can vividly remember my first day of teaching. I was fresh out of college and had signed a contract to teach high school chemistry in a

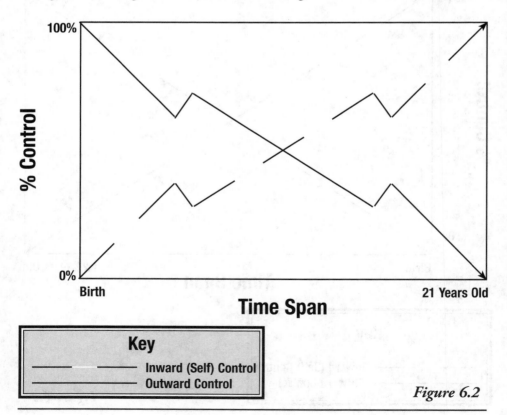

Figure 6.2

public school in New York. Since I had not taken any education courses, I was quite nervous about teaching. The principal of the school had told me that I would be nervous, and therefore, I needed to speak with authority and to be sure to go over my rules with the students right away. I walked into my classroom and found 35 desks sitting ready to receive my students. I was told that I would have approximately 25 students in each class.

The bell rang, signaling the time when the students would start arriving. As these juniors and seniors began walking into the classroom, I made some very interesting observations. Some of these young people were bigger than I was! Some even looked older than I, and several of the boys clearly had been shaving longer than I had. You can imagine my anxiety level rising with each student that entered the classroom.

Soon there were 25 students in the room. I went to close the door, only to be confronted with more students coming in. Now all 35 desks had bodies sitting in them. Surely this would be all of the students, but no, more kept coming through the door. When the tardy bell rang, I stood at the front of the room facing 49 students who seemed to be eagerly waiting to test the skills of this new, young teacher.

In panic, I remembered the words of my principal. In a very loud and demanding voice, I told the class that in the future if they were not in their seats when the bell rang that they should leave and go straight to the office. Of course, I did not even have enough desks in the room for this to happen. Immediately, I began to seat the students alphabetically in the classroom. "If your last name begins with A, start up here," I yelled. Then I proceeded to the Bs, Cs, and so forth until all the students were seated somewhere in the room (this meant some were seated in windowsills and on tables).

It was then time to go over my class rules. I handed out copies of these rules and began going over them in a loud, stern voice. I did this until the bell rang and then dismissed the class, warning them that they must exit the room single file and in an orderly manner. When they had left, I thought to myself, "Teaching is going to be easy. I am good at this. After all I have just controlled 49 students, and no one even said anything the entire class period."

I repeated this procedure for the next two periods with the same results. During lunch, the French teacher came to my room. She asked how I was doing, and I told her that everything was going extremely well.

I then asked her what her morning had been like. She responded, "I have been counseling students not to drop chemistry all morning!" I soon realized that I had focused so much on the rules that I had not even asked the students their names. Their response was one of rebellion. They wanted out of my class.

The next day I began class by first asking each student his/her name. You can imagine my surprise when a student whose last name was Snyder was sitting where the Ds were supposed to be. This student told me that she sat there because I said for the Ds to sit there, and there was no one with a last name beginning with a D. Because of fear, she sat there so I wouldn't get mad. Rules without relationships breed rebellion.

The second principle is of equal importance. If I lose my temper and correct out of anger, I end up assassinating a relationship. Of course, when this happens, I am back in the situation where I have rules without relationships. Parents and teachers must develop strong relationships with their children. Children will not rebel against our rules if those close relationships are in place. However, when we must correct, we cannot afford to do so in anger. If we do so, we will assassinate those relationships that are so important in training our children.

In closing this chapter, let me share with you something my pastor taught us one Sunday. He said that all parents must give their children the things they *need* and not the things they *want*. He went on to share from Scripture that every child has three basic needs. Parents must provide their children

1. Christ-like affection
2. Spirit-guided direction
3. Biblically-based correction

The training process is a demanding one. It is also a very rewarding one when we follow God's plan. Kingdom education begins in the home and is the primary responsibility of parents. God's ideal is that both parents be involved in the education of their children. Too often, the task is left to mom, as dad provides for the family. However, providing the best God has to offer our children requires both mom and dad. When parents begin to fulfill their responsibilities in God's plan for educating future generations, then God will bring others alongside to assist in the process.

7

FINDING HELP

The greatest gift we can give our children is the gift of teachers,
both at home and at school, who teach from a biblical worldview.[1]
Glen Schultz

Before I close this section of the book, I want to share some personal insights for parents as they try to find help in educating their children. Undoubtedly, you have heard the saying that it takes a village to raise a child. This is not true from God's perspective. The home is all that is really necessary to raise a child. Yet the majority of parents will not educate their children totally by themselves. At one time or another, all parents will develop relationships with others who will assist them in training their children.

All parents are home schoolers, training their children at home to some degree. More and more Christian parents are deciding to home school their children on a full-time basis. These parents believe that God has given them the total responsibility to see to it that their children are educated according to biblical principles. Therefore, they are making the necessary sacrifices to ensure that this process is carried out in the home.

Even though the number of full-time home school families is growing, a vast number of parents will choose partners outside the home to assist them in educating their children. Christian parents are very concerned about who should assist or partner with them in this educational task. However, few are paying careful attention to certain fundamental principles when selecting these partners. Of course, most Christian parents are careful in selecting some of the help that they need. For example, we prayerfully seek God's direction when we determine what church our family will attend. But the selection of a church is only one aspect to consider when finding help in training our children.

God's Word provides Christians with some wonderful principles to use when finding help with the education of our children. Several passages caution Christians about allowing *false teachers* or *false doctrine* to influence us and our children.

Recently I have been meditating on Psalm 1, a passage that many Christians memorized as children in Sunday School. The truths found in this short passage have stirred my heart in a fresh and profound way.

> *How happy is the man who does not follow the advice of the*
> *wicked, or take the path of sinners, or join a group of mockers!*
> *(Ps. 1:1, HCSB).*

This one verse makes it clear that God does not want Christians to follow the advice, counsel, or instruction of the wicked. It also sets forth a progression that takes place if a person follows the instruction of the ungodly. If I listen to the advice of the wicked, I will eventually take the path of unrighteousness. In other words, my lifestyle will be similar to that of an unsaved person, and I will be prone to actually joining those who mock and scorn God.

As I contemplated this strong admonition from God, I wondered, who are the wicked? If I am to avoid their advice, I need to know who they are. Sometimes Christians think of the wicked as those of the vilest behavior—murderers, rapists, or child molesters. However, God's Word gives us a clear description of the wicked: "The wicked in his proud countenance does not seek after God; God is in none of his thoughts" (Ps. 10:4, NKJV).

Who are the wicked whose advice we are to shun? They are those who are proud, do not seek God, and have no room for God in their thoughts The wicked are those individuals who live their lives as if God doesn't exist. They may be the people who live right next door. On the surface they may seem pretty much like you and me, but their belief system or worldview is diametrically opposed to God and His ways. We are not to listen to or take advice or teaching from these people.

Since this is true for me, it is also pertinent to consider when I choose who will instruct my children. As a parent I dare not place my children under instruction directed by those who do not seek God and who have no room for Him in their thoughts. Instead, I should do everything in my power to see to it that my children are constantly under the Lord's instruction. My goal should be for my children to find delight in God's Word and have a desire to meditate on it day and night. This is a challenging concept for me to grasp.

This passage of Scripture has far-reaching impact on how Christian parents are to raise their children. Too often we only apply this instruction to what takes place at home and church. We seldom try to apply it to the education we give our children or to other so-called secular aspects of life. However, this Psalm must be applied to all the instruction that our children are given. Christian parents must ask some important questions. Who is teaching and giving advice to our children in school? In textbooks? In school curriculum? In sports activities? In the media they watch and listen to? Our answers can't be found from human opinions and traditions of society. They must be consistent with God's Word.

We find a similar warning in 2 John 10. Here the writer warns Christians not to allow any doctrine that is contrary to the doctrine of Christ into their homes. It makes it clear that if parents welcome the wrong influences into their homes, they will actually share in evil works.

Once we determine in our hearts to apply this passage to all of life, we must be willing to make whatever decisions necessary to ensure that our children are under godly instruction throughout all of their formal education. Knowing the truth of Psalm 1 is the easy part. Actually putting it into practice becomes very difficult—especially when it comes to the education of our children.

My mind once again turns to the recent court ruling that the pledge of allegiance to the country's flag is unconstitutional. Remember this ruling was handed down because of two small words in the pledge—*under God.* While reaction to this ruling has been swift and forceful, we shouldn't be so surprised about this court decision. Is this not the result of decades of secular humanist education that has constantly declared that God doesn't exist and therefore any reference to Him should be removed from public life?

When evolution is taught as a fact of science, students will begin to believe that the supernatural is a myth. Consider how generation after generation of our children has been taught according to the philosophies of relativism, subjectivism, and tolerance. These teachings demand that all beliefs are of equal value and must be esteemed true. They also declare that no one belief, including a belief in God, can be considered universally true for all people.

There is no question that these false philosophies have permeated secular education, dominated media presentations, and directed political policy making. However, the majority of Christian parents and church leaders continue to place their children under the influence of this type of teaching. It is time for Christians to heed the words of the psalmist and delight in the Lord's instruction for both ourselves and our children. Before we stone the judges, we need to search our hearts and repent of our sin of educating our children according to the ways of man and contrary to God's instruction.

Another passage beneficial to Christian parents is found in Exodus 18. In some ways, Moses was trying to educate the entire nation of Israel. It was an awesome responsibility. God had caused Moses to spend 40 years on the backside of a mountain to develop the character he would need to accomplish the work God had for him. Through this humbling experience, Moses had learned to know and trust God in every aspect of life. God then invited Moses to be part of one of the most spectacular works that had ever been done since the creation of the world. God chose Moses to lead Israel out of the land of bondage and into the promised land.

On the journey, Moses tried to get his people to put their trust in God as he himself had earlier learned to do. Moses gave it his all. Each day, he would sit from dawn to dusk and teach the Israelites about God. Jethro, Moses' father-in-law, came to visit Moses and his family. During his visit an interesting thing took place. When Jethro accompanied Moses one day, he was overwhelmed by what Moses was trying to do by himself. He asked Moses, "What is this thing that thou doest to the people? why sittest thou thyself alone, and all the people stand by thee from morning unto even?" (Ex. 18:14, KJV) Moses' response was truthful. He replied, "Because the people come unto me to inquire of God: When they have a matter, they come unto me; and I judge between one and another, and I do make them know the statutes of God, and his laws" (KJV).

This is the same type of responsibility God gave to my wife and me when we became parents. We were responsible to bring up our children in the "nurture and admonition of the Lord." I can remember many days when we were exhausted from trying to accomplish this task. We were overwhelmed, much as Moses was back in the wilderness.

Jethro gave Moses some wise counsel. In verse 17, he told Moses that what he was doing was not good. He saw that if Moses continued to try to carry out this responsibility alone, he would wear away. In today's terms, Jethro was telling Moses that he was going to burn out. In fact, he said that when Moses burned out, so would all the people. Teaching the people about God was too much for one person to tackle by himself. Moses needed help.

It is interesting to see how Jethro's advice to Moses has led to all sorts of applications to the business world. The whole concept of delegation of authority is rooted in this one passage of Scripture. I learned in leadership courses how I was to delegate some of my responsibilities to others. Even the ratios that Jethro presented to Moses are used as measuring sticks today. Many business leaders today will try to limit the number of individuals that report directly to them to ten—the number that Jethro suggested to his son-in-law.

I have been faced with many heavy responsibilities in life. As a school teacher, I was responsible for approximately 100 students each year in my science classes. When I became a high school principal, I was responsible for over 400 students, plus the faculty. Then I became a superintendent, and the responsibility for 1400 students and 120 faculty and staff landed on my desk. I also served as a singles' pastor where I ministered to 100+ single adults. God allowed me to serve for several years as the Southeast Regional Director for the Association of Christian Schools International. While there, I was responsible for serving over 600 schools and 130,000 students in eight states. Today, I am responsible for directing the efforts of a new work within the Southern Baptist Convention to Christian schools and home schools around the world. Each of these tasks was too great for me to do by myself. I had to choose others to assist me.

However, all of these responsibilities combined pale in comparison to the responsibility God gave me as the father of three children. This task is, by far, the most overwhelming load that I have ever carried in life. Just as I could not accomplish my other tasks without proper help, I could not educate and train my children without some assistance. Of course, this responsibility was shared by my wife. I thank God that He made it clear to me very early that the most important decision I could make in life, outside of accepting Jesus as my Lord and Savior, was to marry a godly woman. In this sense, I actually began selecting the assistance I would need in raising children at the moment I decided to ask Sharon to be my wife for all of life.

You are probably saying to yourself right now, "This is good, but how do I know who to choose outside my family and my church to help me educate my children?" I believe the answer is found in this same passage of Scripture. Jethro did more than tell Moses that he had to delegate some of his responsibility to others. Jethro also told his son-in-law to be sure to select people with certain qualifications. It is this step that has been too long overlooked within the Christian home and church. Listen to Jethro's words:

You must be the people's representative before God and bring their disputes to him. Teach them the decrees and laws, and show them the way to live and the duties they are to perform. But select capable men from all the people—men who fear God, trustworthy men who hate dishonest gain—*and appoint them as officials over thousands, hundreds, fifties, and tens (Ex. 18:19-21, NIV, emphasis mine).*

The King James Version lists three qualifications for those who could assist Moses with his God-given responsibilities. Moses needed men who

1. Feared God
2. Loved truth
3. Hated covetousness

As parents, Sharon and I have tried to follow this principle as we have attempted to educate our children. We have tried always to choose others who met these three qualifications to help in training our children. Sometimes parents have told me that they didn't have the freedom to choose who would help them with this task. I disagree. No one can take that freedom away from me; I can only choose to give that freedom away. As we have carefully chosen those who would assist us with our children's development, certain prices have had to be paid. In some instances, we had to make changes because a teacher in a Sunday School class was not teaching God's truth. We have also had to sacrifice material possessions to pay the extra cost of ensuring that our children's school teachers met these qualifications personally and in what they taught in the classroom. It is imperative that parents assume the responsibility of choosing only godly help in educating their children. One Christian leader puts it this way.

Parents must involve themselves in their children's lives enough to insure that *no other influence* takes precedence. ... Whenever outside influences shape a child's character more than parents, the parents have failed in their duties. ... Before the throne of God *we* will be held accountable if we have turned our children over to other influences that shape their character in ungodly ways.[2]

Now that our children are grown and on their own, we realize that we have been spared many heartaches because we followed the principles laid out in this portion of God's Word. Chuck Swindoll in his book *Stress Fractures* refers to this passage as one of the keys to avoiding the fractures in life that come from the stress of carrying out one's God-given responsibilities.[3]

In summarizing this section, it is evident that the home plays the most important role in kingdom education. We have discussed four key principles in this section:

1. Parents have been given the assignment to raise godly offspring.
2. The training process (education) must be based on truth.
3. The end goal of this assignment is to raise children who know Jesus Christ as Savior and think and act from a biblical worldview.
4. Parents must choose able men and women who "fear God, love truth, and hate covetousness" to help them with this assignment.

As we consider that kingdom education is God's plan for educating future generations, we must consistently obey the biblical principles God has given us so that we can be successful in this all-important role as parents.

Section III

KINGDOM EDUCATION:

THE ROLE

OF THE CHURCH

8

THE IMPORTANCE OF THE CHURCH

The church is the body of Christ.
He is the Head of the church, and it exists to do His work in the world.[1]
Gene Mims

The church is vitally important to God, but before one can understand the church's importance, he must first understand something about God's kingdom. Two phrases are used in reference to this kingdom. It is sometimes referred to as the kingdom of heaven. Both John the Baptist and Christ preached the same message, "Repent for the kingdom of heaven is at hand."

Other times this kingdom is referred to as the kingdom of God. In Matthew 6, Jesus talked about the kingdom of God, as did Paul in Romans 14. There has been some controversy as to just what *is* the kingdom of God. Is it something that will become a reality in the future, or is it something that exists right now? The people of Jesus' day thought it would be an actual physical kingdom that would be a political alternative to Roman government. Paul, on the other hand, said that it is more than a physical reign. He said it is a spiritual reign that could be experienced during our life on earth.

We defined the kingdom of God earlier in this book as the "reign of God through Jesus Christ in the lives of persons as evidenced by God's activity in, through, and around them."[2] According to this definition, we see that God's kingdom is something that is both present and active today. The present reality of God's kingdom is the highest priority that God desires in the life of every believer. Matthew 6:33 states, "Seek first the kingdom of God and His righteousness." (NKJV). Above all else, God wants you and me to seek His kingdom.

The kingdom of God is the broadest view of what God is doing to accomplish His will throughout His creation. Within this kingdom, God has ordained the church to play a significant role. We are familiar with Christ's words: "Upon this rock I will build my church; and the gates of hell shall not prevail against it" (Matt. 16:18, KJV). The church is referred to as the bride of Christ. There is no question that God has set the church in a very strategic position of great importance to His kingdom work.

Jesus gave His life for the church. Because of this tremendous truth, we must recognize the value of the church in God's eyes. In Colossians 1:18, we find that Christ has been placed as the Head of the church so that He might have the preeminence in all things. As individual believers, we make up the various parts or members of the church. First Corinthians 12 uses the analogy of the physical body for the church. Christians are the fingers, the eyes, and the other members of God's spiritual body. However, we must never forget that Christ, alone, is the Head.

Even though the church is made up of all believers, God has instituted the concept of local church congregations through which His will is accomplished. From the day of Pentecost forward, we find God emphasizing the importance of all believers being involved in the local church. In Ephesians 4:11, Paul explained how God uses people in different roles, some as evangelists and others as pastors and teachers, in order to strengthen and edify the church. Paul was chief among those who started local churches. In Acts 2:46-47, we find that believers continued daily in fellowship with other believers through a local church. The church will be described in more detail in chapter 10.

God's Word emphasizes that one day Jesus will return to take His church to be with Him for all eternity. In several passages of Scripture we find an emphasis on the importance of the church being ready for the Lord's return. The inference is clear that the church is to be blameless and pure so that she will be fit for the Bridegroom when He comes for her. This principle is important to keep in mind as we discuss kingdom education and its relationship to the church.

If, indeed, kingdom education has as its major focus the goal of making disciples and preparing them for the coming of the Lord, then the church must maintain a *priority position* in any educational efforts that claim to be

Christian. And as Christians are being properly educated, they will see the need to become members of local church congregations. They will not only become members but will also desire to be useful within the church. Believers will understand that each person has certain abilities and gifts that are to be used effectively within the church. Unfortunately, more and more Christians today do not identify with a local church, and even more do not use their spiritual gifts within the church. We have become a generation of observers and not participants in the local church. Kingdom education will build the church and not undermine it through inactivity.

Statistics show that only 30 percent of youth in churches have taken ownership of their faith by the time they graduate from high school.[3] According to Burkett, "A large evangelical denomination recently reported that if they had been successful at just one evangelical outreach—that of their own children—their denomination would be four times larger than it is today."[4] The church plays an important role in kingdom education.

Today most organizations know that it is very important to operate from a specific purpose statement in order to succeed in accomplishing their goals and objectives. When God determined to organize His people in the church, He established a specific purpose statement by which His organization was to function. It is found in Matthew 28:18-20. Here Jesus declared

> *All authority has been given to Me in heaven and on earth. Go therefore and make disciples of all the nations, baptizing them in the name of the Father and of the Son and of the Holy Spirit, teaching them to observe all things that I have commanded you; and lo, I am with you always, even to the end of the age (NKJV).*

This purpose statement of the church is not to be looked upon as a *suggestion* to consider in its everyday operations. Instead, it is to be the driving force by which the church operates and by which it is to evaluate everything the church undertakes. Finally, it is to be the ultimate ruler by which we measure and evaluate each and every program attempted by the church. Kingdom education must be structured and practiced so that this purpose will be of highest priority.

9

THE GREAT COMMISSION

The church is a kingdom agent, the bridge between
a gracious God and lost humanity.[1]
Gene Mims

We have just examined some very important points about the church that must be considered as we try to understand God's plan for educating future generations. Let me summarize these points for you.

- The kingdom of God is the highest priority for every Christian.
- The kingdom of God provides us with the broadest view of what God is doing in the world today.
- The church has been ordained as the expression of God's kingdom to the world.
- Individual Christians are members of the church, but Jesus Christ is the Head and is to have preeminence in the church.
- Christians are to become active members of local church congregations.
- The Great Commission is the purpose statement that must drive all that takes place within and through the church.

When we take a careful look at the Great Commission, it becomes extremely clear that education plays a very strong and critical role in its fulfillment.

The church has one assignment and that is to make disciples. When the church is making disciples, it must be certain to make disciples of Jesus Christ. Many times we attempt to make disciples of a church, of a denomination, or even of a church leader. Jesus gave us this assignment according to His authority. His authority is complete and all-encompassing. Not only did He give this command by His authority, but He also promised that His authority would stay with us until the end of this age. As long as our emphasis is on making disciples of Jesus Christ, Jesus will give us the authority to accomplish this mission successfully.

Let us review the model that was presented earlier in this book concerning the definition of kingdom education. A kingdom-focused education must be founded upon:

1. Jesus Christ
2. A Biblical Philosophy of Education
3. Evangelism
4. Discipleship

We find these same core truths at the center of the Great Commission. This purpose statement for the church has three major functions, which are

1. Conversion
2. Identification with Christ
3. Teaching

In Matthew 28:19, Christ exhorts Christians to go and make disciples. The word *go* carries with it the meaning of continuous effort. It might be translated as "in your going, continuously make disciples." The purpose of the church is to be daily sharing the good news of the saving grace of Jesus Christ. The evangelization of lost people is to be at the center of all a church does. One might ask the question, "Where does this statement mention evangelism or salvation?" It only talks about making disciples. One can never become a disciple of Jesus Christ until he or she first knows Him as personal Savior. Therefore, conversion is absolutely necessary in order for one to become a disciple.

When one knows Christ as Savior, it is then necessary for that individual to develop a personal identity with Jesus. This is what it means to be a disciple. A true disciple of Christ will think and act in a manner fitting to the mind of Christ, Himself. The process of becoming a disciple of Christ is very similar to that of being conformed to His image. It is a lifelong process that will never reach completion until we are with Him in heaven for all eternity. However, we must continuously be making progress toward full identification with Christ.

The third function found in this purpose statement for the church is that of teaching. One cannot be a disciple merely by accepting Christ as Savior and identifying with Him through baptism and church membership. The test of discipleship is obedience to His commands. Knowing what Christ has commanded of us does not come naturally. We must be taught to *do*, not just to *know* what He has commanded. Too few Christians are being made into disciples in today's church. They are somewhat like the little boy who fell out of bed in the middle of the night. When his parents rushed in and asked him what happened, he responded, "I guess I fell asleep too close to where I got in." Too many Christians are falling into sin because they have fallen asleep too close to where they have gotten into the church.

God wants His children to know Him in a personal way. However, this only happens as we are taught God's Word in a way that will transform our lives into being His disciples. The teaching of God's Word is extremely important in fulfilling the church's purpose statement. The reason for this is found in 2 Timothy 3:16-17:

> *All Scripture is given by inspiration of God, and is profitable for doctrine, for reproof, for correction, for instruction in righteousness, that the man of God may be complete, thoroughly equipped for every good work (NKJV).*

God expects His disciples to be equipped to do His good works daily, regardless of the circumstances in which we find ourselves. Living out what God's Word teaches is the only way that we can become equipped in this manner.

Notice the four ways we can profit from knowing God's Word. We can first find profit in doctrine, then it is profitable for reproof, next it profits us through correction, and, finally, we profit through instruction in righteousness. Understanding the meaning of these four aspects of instruction will help us focus our teaching on the proper things as we are involved in kingdom education. Consider the following correlations.

Doctrine. . . . . What's Right
Reproof . . . . What's Wrong
Correction . . . . How To Get Right
Instruction In Righteousness . . . . How To Stay Right

God's Word provides us with instruction in how to live successful lives as His disciples. Someone else has explained these areas of God's Word as what we should do, what we shouldn't do, what we should stop doing, and what we should continue to do. No matter how we look at these verses, it is clear that teaching must be an important function of the local church if we are to successfully carry out the purpose statement set forth in the Great Commission.

Understanding the purpose statement for the church is vital to understanding the importance of kingdom education to the church. The church must give careful attention and support to kingdom education issues. Each of the three functions described in the Great Commission involves education. Evangelism points people to Jesus Christ as the only way to eternal life. Discipleship involves the believer's efforts to identify with Jesus Christ. Teaching becomes the methodology used to accomplish the task of making disciples.

10

SUPPORTING THE HOME

Family life today is like walking through a dangerous mine field.
The church needs to help families not merely survive but to thrive.[1]
Billie Friel

It has been said that the strength of the home will determine the strength of the church. Since the church is made up of families, the church can be no stronger than the families who attend and are a part of the church. Church leaders must pay careful attention to the role they have in developing and supporting the home. Every effort needs to be made to strengthen the spiritual tenor of the family. A recent report from the Southern Baptist Convention Committee on Family Life said that pastors and church leaders must be enabled to identify and hold forth "'key biblical principles for marriage and family.'"[2] Once again, this involves education.

I believe most parents want to be good parents and to have a strong home. Josh McDowell recently stated to me that the number one item in a youth pastor's job description should be training parents how to parent. This could be said for children's pastors, ministers of education, and, to some degree, senior pastors.

One young father wrote Dr. John MacArthur and asked for help.

> I'm looking for *biblical* help with parenting. Not just parenting advice from a Christian perspective, not just warmed-over child psychology couched in "Christian" terminology, but solid, biblical parenting guidelines.[3]

Today's parents are struggling to discover the secrets of being good parents. They have grown up watching the American home disintegrate before their eyes. Gaebelein made a disturbing observation more than 50 years ago: "Once the home with grace at meals, family prayers, and loyalty to the church, could to a significant degree be counted upon to provide children with a spiritual heritage."[4] However, this is no longer the case. I believe that we have seen several generations of parents try to raise godly children having never been given solid training on what it takes to be a biblical parent. Oh, we have conducted seminars on communication, relationships, and discipline, but we never deal with the fundamental principles of parenting.

Barna reports that only 33 percent of born again parents claimed that church and faith were important influences on their parenting ideas and actions. . . Only one half of born again parents mentioned anything related to their faith (including the Bible, church, or religion) as a significant influence on how they raise their children.[5] The church must step up to the plate and help today's parents understand what the Bible says about raising godly offspring.

Most churches offer programs that will meet various needs within the home. There are fellowship times for all ages planned throughout the year. There are studies on everything from life courses to weight loss programs taking place on a regular basis. There are many types of support groups being developed. All of these programs are designed to help individuals and families cope with the many pressures facing them.

However, very little is being done to help parents understand the kingdom education principles that have been addressed in this book. Sometimes the lack of such teaching and preaching results from a lack of understanding of these issues by the leaders of the church. Unfortunately, sometimes educational issues are avoided because of pressures, either real or perceived, from various groups and/or individuals within the church. Pastors feel as if they are in a no-win situation when it comes to addressing issues related to education.

PRESSURES ON THE PASTOR

When parents ask a church leader where they should send their children to school, the leader thinks that any answer he might give is likely to offend someone in the church. Those who home school pressure pastors to encourage other parents to do as they do. Others who teach in Christian schools expect the pastor to support this type of education, while those in public education become offended if the pastor would in any way encourage parents to remove their children from public schools. Pastors believe they cannot give much support to Christian schools because they have some fine Christians who are teachers and administrators in the public schools. They explain that these individuals would consider it a slap in the face if the pastor were to support other forms of education.

Church leaders must come to grips with the reality that kingdom education deals with *how* God wants us to educate our children and not with *where* He calls His mature disciples to serve Him. The involvement of the church in helping the home educate their children in no way negates God's call on men and women to serve in secular educational institutions. There is a need for godly men and women to be *salt and light* in all areas of education. However, in the Sermon on the Mount, Jesus gave this challenge to His disciples, not to children and youth. Whenever Jesus talked about children, He always did so in reference to their nurturing and protection.

Faced with these pressures, most church leaders simply ignore the issue completely, but the issue does not go away. Instead, the home finds no support from the church in one of the most crucial areas of influence in children's and young peoples' lives. The home and the church must join forces and turn back to God's Word for clear instruction on how to educate our children. In *Education in a Democracy*, Dr. Frank Gaebelein portrayed the youth of America as headed for trouble.

> The fact is that, as both home and church have lost grip on American youth, the people of this country have looked to education to fill the gap. With a confidence that would be touching were it not based on evasion of responsibility, they have turned their youth—body, mind, and soul—over to the most extensive and highly organized system of education this world has even known.[6]

The church must provide godly counsel, instruction, and supporting programs in matters concerning education if it is going to strengthen the home and, in turn, strengthen the effectiveness of the church. Instead of pastors and other church leaders supporting public, Christian, or home schools, they need to teach parents the biblical principles of kingdom education (see Appendix). Once these principles are presented and parents begin to obey them, it will be necessary for the church to offer resources, programs, and services that will support these parents in their effort to provide biblically-based, Christ-centered education to their children.

Why must the church pay attention to the education of children? "Research suggests that 70 percent of teens involved in a youth group will have stopped attending church within two years of their high school graduation. It's a devastating problem for parents and for the church."[7] Jay Strack, a leading youth evangelist, recently stated that the percentage of 18-year-olds that are leaving the church has risen to 88 percent.[8] The church cannot ignore this reality. It can be argued that this trend may be taking place because our young people have developed a secular mindset by the time they leave high school. If this is true, and I believe it is, the church must assume greater leadership in reinforcing the principles of kingdom education taught in the home.

If the church does not assist the home in discipling our children toward godliness, we will *inoculate* them against the things of God. Wilkinson drives this point home with intensity.

> In the medical field, inoculation is when the doctor gives you enough of the germs, usually the flu, to help your body build up a resistance to the disease. Christians can spiritually inoculate their children against the things of God by giving them just enough of the rules and regulations without sharing the joy and vibrancy of the Holy Spirit. The children learn that God is real but church is boring and Christianity is a series of rules to follow. They become resistant to the things of God.[9]

Church leaders cannot afford to be neutral on the issue of educating future generations. Pastors must become bold and help parents understand what is at stake spiritually when it comes to educating their children.

THE REDEFINING OF THE CHURCH

The church is described in Acts 2 as a dynamic body of believers that met daily. This passage also gives clear indication that the home was very much involved in the church. The same concept of the church was evident in the early days of the United States. As church and home were intricately linked to one another, their combined influence on government, education, and society was extraordinary.

However, in the 1800s something took place that had a profound effect on the church and, ultimately, on society. We have already studied how the church relinquished its control over the formal education of children during this time. When the church separated itself from the education of children and youth, it forfeited the opportunity to have a strong influence on the spiritual transformation of future generations. The church's role in education became trying to counteract the negative impact of a secular educational system. What has happened is that "we have privatized our religion as we have secularized our culture."[10]

Since the mid 1800's, the church has been redefined as something that primarily takes place on Sundays and on Wednesday nights. This definition has become so engrained that whenever one speaks about the church, he immediately thinks about Sunday worship or Wednesday night prayer meetings. In fact, seminaries and schools of religion train church leaders how to do *Sunday and Wednesday night church*. The result is that the church has lost its influence on public life. Whenever, it tries to assert itself as a moral agent in society, the cry for separation of church and state is raised.

The result of redefining of the church has been devastating to say the least. Dr. Gene Mims, president of LifeWay Church Resources, challenged me to consider five questions that he sees every Christian and non-Christian adult struggling to answer. As I studied them, I saw them as five life-drive needs.

1. How can I find spiritual fulfillment in life?
2. How can I develop meaningful, lasting relationships—especially in marriage and the family?
3. How can I successfully raise or educate my children?
4. How can I find meaning in work?
5. How can I fit in or make sense out of my community/world?

Questions came to my mind concerning these life-drive needs. Are there answers to each of these life-drives? Are there any over-arching solutions that bring them into meaningful relationships with one another? Where does a Christian find solutions to these life dilemmas? Who will teach us how to find answers and purpose in each of these areas of life and in life in general? These are all extremely critical questions for these turbulent times.

The common response given to many of them is that answers to all of life are found in the person of Jesus Christ. The Bible, God's Word, is the only place where the answers can be found. It is absolutely true that in Christ one will find the only true meaning for life, but if that is all there is to it, why are so many Christians still struggling and failing in many, if not all, of these life-drive areas?

Christians struggle with making sense out of life in these areas just as much as lost people do, but you and I must realize that there are only two sources for possible solutions to our life-drive needs. These two sources give people answers that are in total opposition to each other, yet there can only be one source that can provide true answers for every life-drive need.

People try to find answers to life either from God or from the world. It is vital to realize that both God and the world will tell people how to find purpose in life. Every person turns to one or the other of these two sources to try to make sense out of his or her life. Even Christians struggle with the question *Which source has the real answers to life's biggest questions?* So we must compare how God's ways and the world's ways conflict in each life-drive area. (See Figure 10.1.)

The sad reality is that more and more Christians seem to be following the answers the world gives rather than those given by the church. Why? I become more convinced each day that it is because the church has been assigned to a Sunday-Wednesday night "box" and most church leaders and members have accepted this new definition of church.

The church has access to most of its members for only 2-4 hours each week, while the world, especially through education and the media, has 24-7 access to our lives. Because of this inequity, the world has been more effective in influencing our beliefs about these major life issues than the church. If the church is going to be the agent of spiritual transformation that God intends it to be, it must become much more active in the everyday lives of its members, especially parents. It is time for churches to expand their ministries to include biblical education for children and youth throughout the week.

Life-drive	God's Ways	World's Ways
Spiritual Fulfillment	A person can only find spiritual fulfillment in the person of Jesus Christ (John 14:6). Spiritual maturity can only be achieved when one's personal relationship with Christ is characterized by love, trust, and obedience to Him.	All religions lead to the same end. Therefore, each person must find what works best for him. Christianity may be fine for some but it is not for everyone. Some people will discover that they themselves are divine and can find meaning from within.
Marriage & Family	God ordained marriage as the most important human relationship (Genesis 2). His ideal for marriage can be summed up in the absolute "I love you for life!" The marriage relationship is to be an earthly picture of the heavenly reality of the relationship between Jesus and His church. Christ is to be preeminent in the home if the home is to be all that God intends it to be.	The new absolute to follow in marriage is "I love you for now!" If the marriage is not working for you, end it and try again. Keep trying until you find a relationship that is best for you. One can measure success in the home by the type of house you own, the number of cars you drive, and the kind of neighborhood you live in.
Educating Children	Children are God's homework assignment to parents. He expects every parent to follow the instructions in Scripture on how to educate children. The goals of true education are for each child to know Christ as Lord and Savior and to serve Christ in life from a biblical worldview.	A "good" education will cause children to become happy, productive citizens who will value diversity and tolerate (honor) every person's values as being equal to their own. The goals of education are to perfect the individual and thus society and to achieve financial success in this life.
Purpose in Work	God gives unique talents and abilities to each person He creates. God's plan is for each person to develop those abilities and accept God's call on his life to use them to "subdue the world" in a way that will bring glory to Him.	You can be anything you want to be if you just work hard enough. To be successful in work, you must climb the corporate ladder. If you don't feel fulfilled, put more time and energy into your career. You have rights, Only be loyal to yourself, and Be your own boss are values that you must believe in to be successful.
The World	God created man as a living soul and therefore as a social being needing fellowship with others in everyday life. One realizes that, as a Christian, he is a stranger in this world because he is a citizen of heaven, a peculiar person. He also has a responsibility to love this world of people like God does.	Every person is "created" equal and this includes one's beliefs and values. Therefore, each person must be tolerant and accept as his equal every other person and his values. Acceptance of cultural diversity is the solution to strife in any community. There must be "equality" in the economic and social environments for all people. It is possible if this occurs that all people will live together in social harmony.

Figure 10.1

THE IMPORTANCE OF MARRIAGE

Since parents have the primary responsibility for educating their children, it is of utmost importance that the home remain strong. To educate children properly requires, whenever possible, both parents. Therefore, the church must concentrate more on teaching men and women how important marriage and the home is to the Lord. Marriage must be a visible focus of both preaching and teaching. And leaders must not only teach, but also model, what it is to have a Christ-centered home and how a godly husband and wife are to relate to one another. When this takes place, fathers and mothers will be better prepared to begin training their children in the nurture and admonition of the Lord.

A TEACHING PLAN IS IMPERATIVE

Finally, the church leadership must develop a teaching plan to assist parents in educating their children according to biblical principles. This would be a good time for church leaders to go back and review the material found in chapters two through seven. In these chapters, pastors and other church leaders will find principles that must be taught to all families within their churches. There will be some risk involved in following such a course of action. Some will accuse the church and its leaders of supporting one form of school over another. Regardless of such pressures, the truths of kingdom education must be a vital part of the church's teaching program.

When church leadership instills within its congregation the importance of educating children according to biblical principles, it will strengthen the church. First, parents will assume more responsibility for the proper training of their children. In turn they will become more involved in programs in which their children participate, both at church and at school. Programs within the church will be stronger through the increased interest and participation of more parents.

There can be no greater effort made by churches on behalf of their congregations than to assist them with facing the issues of education as they relate to their children. I am firmly convinced that the future health of the church will depend on the support that churches give the home concerning educational issues. The church must break out of the *Sunday-Wednesday night box* and get back to the concept of the church described in Acts 2. This means that the church will expand its ministry throughout the week—especially in providing biblically-based, Christ-centered education to children and youth. It is time that the church provided support based on the principles undergirding kingdom education rather than on pressures from the various factions of educators attending any given church. Church leaders must never forget the ultimate purpose for the church's existence—to make disciples!

Section IV

11

THE SCHOOL
AND THE HOME

*Parents are realizing that all education is value oriented and that
Christian nurture is a full-time endeavor and are increasingly supporting
schools which embody the biblical beliefs and values of the home.*[1]
James Carper

Since kingdom education is a 24-hour-a-day process, the role of the school
is of vital importance. Even though schools are not mentioned in the Bible,
they have become an integral part of our culture. Schools have existed for
many centuries. In the past, American society had "the habit of looking to
the school to produce a learned piety and patriotism. [This habit] became
so deeply ingrained in the American mind that few questioned its validity."[2]
Christians have always placed a high value on education, especially in the
United States. When the Massachusetts Colony was established in 1647, the
colonists adopted the Massachusetts School Act. The primary purpose of
this act was to ensure that children would be educated to such a degree that
they would be able to have a knowledge of the Scriptures. In fact, this act
required every town of 50 families to establish an elementary school.

The *General Laws and Liberties of New Plymouth Colony* were revised in
1671 to include a section entitled "Education of Children."

> Parents and Masters do direly Endeavor, by themselves, or oth-
> ers, to teach their children and servants as they grow capable,
> so much learning as through the blessings of God they may
> attain, at least to be able to read the Scriptures ... and in
> some competent measure to understand the main ground and
> Principles of Christian Religion, necessary to Salvation.[3]

Parents were fined if their children were not so trained. Few would dispute that schools continue to play a very important role in society. But the question being asked today is What role should a school play in training our children?

As early as 1954, Francis Curran sounded the alarm to educators of his day, citing the virtual surrender of the Christian church in America as it relinquished its traditional role of elementary education to the state. The impact of this new direction can hardly be overemphasized, for its effects were quickly seen not only in the church and state, but in the home.

THE RISE OF SECULARIZATION

This development marked the beginning of a major shift in the role of the school in relationship to the home. Until this time, schools were established in order to provide support to the biblical values and beliefs of the home. The school was to enable the child to be able to read the Bible and think from a biblical perspective. As schools became state controlled, the emphasis changed from supporting the values of the home to instilling the values of the government into the lives of the students. Even before court rulings in 1962, 1963, and 1981 declared prayer, Bible reading, and the hanging of the 10 commandments unconstitutional in public schools, the schools were significantly contributing to the secularization of society.

In 1940, Charles Clayton Morrison, former editor of *The Christian Century*, addressed 10,000 public school teachers in Kansas City.

> The public school is confessedly and deliberately secular. I am bound, therefore, to lay on the doorstep of our educational system the prime responsibility for the decline of religion and the steady advance of secularism, another name for atheism, in American society. ... Protestant children in public schools are under an influence which the churches cannot counteract. The public school presents the church with a generation of youth whose minds have been cast in a secular world.[4]

Schools have assumed more and more responsibility in areas of children's lives that should be addressed and handled by the home. We must never forget that God gives the responsibility for the education of one's children not to the state or to the school nor even to the church. He gives this responsibility to parents. Therefore, the school's role must be established as providing *support* to the home. Schools can never replace the home as the primary place where a child's training and education is to take place.

Christian homes must be certain that their children's school is founded on the same biblical principles and values by which their home operates. By choosing a school that holds to their Christian beliefs and values, parents ensure that their children will receive a consistent education both at home and at school. When this takes place, life makes more sense to the child. This concept is evident in the Jewish community. As mentioned in the introduction, the Jewish faith has been sustained in a miraculous way, considering all the persecution that Jews have experienced throughout their history. This did not take place haphazardly. Orthodox Jews make a concerted effort to ensure that the school supports their own beliefs and values. This is why the Jewish boy said, "Life makes sense because what is binding on him was also binding on his father and his teachers."[5]

The Bible gives clear direction as to the place that God and His Word must have in the home. Christ must be the center of the home if the family is going to be what God intends it to be. When the home is functioning according to biblical principles, education will be viewed as a means by which these same principles can be further taught to one's children. Parents will then see the importance of choosing a school that would reinforce what is being taught in the home.

There has been an effort to try to separate values and religion from what takes place in the school. Horace Mann, the father of American public schools, once said that society should leave "the teaching of faith and values to the home and church and the teaching of facts to the schools."[6] However, Hirst noted in 1967 that "whether we like it or not, the whole enterprise of education, from top to bottom, is value-ridden."[7] H. Shelton Smith concluded in his classic study, *Faith and Nurture,*

> The paramount question is this: What kind of religion shall
> the school teach—the religion of the churches or the religion
> of humanistic experimentalism? Sooner or later this must
> become the focal point of a crucial battle. On its outcome
> largely hangs the fate of democratic culture in America.[8]

Parents must realize that there is an all-out war being waged for the minds of their children. Dr. James Dobson made this clear when he wrote

> Nothing short of a great Civil War of Values rages today throughout North America. Two sides with vastly differing and incompatible world-views are locked in a bitter conflict that permeates every level of society. ... Instead of fighting for territory or military conquest, however, the struggle now is for the hearts and minds of the people. It is a war over *ideas*. And someday soon, I believe, a winner will emerge and the loser will fade from memory.[9]

Dobson saw that our children are the targets of the strongest attacks in battles waged in the school classroom. He said, "Children are the prize to the winners of the second great civil war. Those who control what young people are taught and what they experience—what they see, hear, think, and believe—will determine the future course for the nation."[10] Emphasizing the role of education in this civil war, he said, "As we will see, the hottest battles in this civil war are being fought on educational turf, and that is where eventual victory or defeat will occur."[11]

If we do not realize the severity of the war of values in which we are engaged, we will lose our children to this world's system. To emphasize this reality, consider the following statements made by school leaders from the beginning of the common schools in America right through to today.

Horace Mann (father of American public schools, died in 1859):
> We who are engaged in the sacred cause of education are entitled to look upon all parents as having given hostages to our cause.[12]

C. F. Potter (original signer of the first Humanist Manifesto, 1930):
> Education is thus a most powerful ally of humanism, and every American public school is a school of humanism. What can the theistic Sunday Schools, meeting for an hour once a week, and teaching only a fraction of the children, do to stem the tide of a five-day program of humanistic teaching?[13]

Paul Blanshard (liberal author and crusader for social justice, 1976):
I think the most important factor leading us to a secular society has been the educational factor. Our schools may not teach
Johnny to read properly, but the fact that Johnny is in school
until he is 16 tends to lead toward the elimination of religious
superstition. The average child now acquires a high school
education, and this *militates* against Adam and Eve and all
other myths of alleged history (emphasis mine).[14]

Dr. John Goodland (former president of National Education Association):
Our goal is behavioral change. The majority of our youth still
hold to the values of their parents, and if we do not recognize
this pattern, or we do not resocialize them to accept change,
our society may decay.[15]

John Dunphy (from a prize-winning essay in *The Humanist,* 1983):
I am convinced that the battle for humankind's future [the battle for the mind] must be waged and won in the public school
classrooms by teachers who correctly perceive their role as the
proselytizers of a new faith: a religion of humanity that recognizes and respects the spark of what theologians call divinity
in every human being. These teachers must embody the same
selfless dedication as the most rabid fundamentalist preachers,
for they will be ministers of another sort, utilizing a classroom
instead of a pulpit to convey humanist values in whatever subject they teach, regardless of the education level—preschool
day care or large state university.

The classroom must and will become an arena of conflict between
the old and the new—the rotting corpse of Christianity, together
with all its adjacent evils and misery, and the new faith of humanism, resplendent in its promise of world in which the never-realized
Christian ideal of "love thy neighbor" will finally be achieved. ... It
will undoubtedly be a long, arduous, painful struggle replete with
much sorrow and many tears, but humanism will emerge
triumphant. It must if the family of humanity is to survive.[16]

Some would question whether or not these statements accurately describe what is taking place in secular education today in the country. However, a look at some textbooks of the last few decades provides us with ample evidence that the battle is raging far beyond what the average Christian realizes. Consider these excerpts from a few texts.

Economics Today and Tomorrow, Teacher's Edition (high school, 1991)
> Can we say that the growth of government is good or bad? Everyone knows that government in the United States has grown in the 1900s—particularly during the Depression and during the 1960s and 1970s. Can we say whether there is a good or bad society? Is there an answer to such a debate? Not really, because the side that one takes depends on one's values. *No right or wrong answer exists when values are at stake* (emphasis mine).[17]

Psychology for Living (high school, 1971)
> Everyone must develop his own set of principles to govern his own sexual behavior. ... The particular patterns of behavior that one accepts for himself is a decision that adults must make.[18]

Communicating (2nd Grade, 1973)
> The moral has been purposely omitted in order that the children when talking about the story, may come to *their own* conclusions (emphasis mine).[19]

A More Perfect Union (8th Grade, 1991)
> America [has] marveled at the broad diversity of its people. ... prided itself on its ability to accept—and to borrow from—the lifestyles and values of may different nationalities. ... [Pluralism] means that people must compromise ... by yielding on certain points. ... Americans [must] exercise tolerance ... [for the] lifestyles of others.[20]

Psychology for Living (high school, 1971)
> The adjusted individual conforms where it is mutually *beneficial to himself* and society—to laws, to rules of etiquette, to modes of dress, for example. He does not conform when his principles or *his best judgment* advise against it (emphasis mine).[21]

World: Adventures in Time and Place (6th Grade, 2000)
> One of the most important parts of any culture is its values. … Many people's values are shaped by religious beliefs. As a Hindu, for example, Azeez believes that all living things have souls and are "a fraction of God." … Think about how the way you live at home reflects your family's beliefs and customs. … Cultures do not stay the same forever. They constantly change through their interaction with other cultures.[22]

World History, The Human Experience (6th Grade, 1999)
> Evaluate both positive and negative consequences. Make a sound decision about which alternative is *best for you* (emphasis mine).[23]

These excerpts from some of the common textbooks used in schools today present students with subtle messages that slowly shape a secular, man-centered worldview. Some material blatantly attacks absolute truth when making moral choices. For example, *The Quest for Excellence,* a booklet produced to help early teens "achieve an ethical code that belongs to you" states:

> Even if your parents haven't talked to you specifically about sex, you probably have a good idea of how they feel anyway. If your parents are very protective, or if they expect you to be a virgin for the rest of your life, their message may not be very realistic. If they fear your sexuality or don't want you to be sexual at all, you may *feel a need to tune out their voices* (emphasis mine).[24]

There can be no doubt about it—education is playing and will continue to play an important role in this new civil war of values that is aimed at capturing the hearts and minds of future generations. Because of this reality, kingdom education requires that the school be a support for the Christian home and that the beliefs and values taught in the school must reinforce those that God says must be taught and practiced in the home. If this does not happen, our children's lives will become more and more fragmented, and life will continue to lose purpose and meaning. To be a part of kingdom education, schools must have their instruction grounded in God's Word. When this is not the case, according to Philip May, author of *Which Way to Educate*, and "man or man's reason, is the measure of all things, then absolute standards as the Christian thinks of them cease to exist."[25]

This is exactly what is believed in today's postmodern culture. May predicted that this would take place because "those who reject the Christian faith have to accept other 'authorities,' such as self, power, reason, or consensus of expert or mass opinion."[26] As we illustrated in chapter 2, May based this prediction on his conviction that only Christianity can provide a Bible-based worldview, and it is precisely this worldview that undergirds the standards, goals and purpose of kingdom education. May's bold statement was and is right on point.

The school becomes an extension of the home when parents are involved in God's plan for educating future generations. Kingdom education principles apply to what takes place in the classroom in the same way they apply to what is taught and practiced in the home. Parents must be certain to choose schools that will reinforce the biblical beliefs and values that they want instilled in their children's hearts and minds.

Schools which are founded on these biblical principles must never forget their supportive role to the Christian home. Without this cooperative commitment to the truths of God's Word between the home and the school, kingdom education ceases to be a reality. Psalm 78 paints a vivid picture of what takes place when the education of children is not carried out consistently in all aspects of life. In verses 1-7, we find God's instruction to parents and the nation of Israel about what they need to teach their children. In verses 8-64 God describes the suffering and moral collapse that took place because His people did not follow His instructions and train their children properly. These verses underscore the urgent need for the Christian home and the school to work together along with the church to educate children according to principles of kingdom education.

12

THE SCHOOL AND THE CHURCH

If the church withdraws from one division of education,
the logical consequence will be the ultimate abandonment
of all formal education by the church.[1]
Francis Curran

Any school that is involved in kingdom education must give careful attention to its relationship with the church. We must never forget that the church is the expression of God's Kingdom to the lost world. The church is the instrument through which God desires Christians to carry out the Great Commission. Therefore, schools must relate closely to the church. This is true for any Christian school, whether it is church-sponsored or independent board-operated.

Unfortunately today, many schools and churches do not have the harmonious relationships that are needed for kingdom education to be effective. Many pastors and other church leaders do not support the efforts being made by Christian schools in their communities. Some churches that sponsor schools are embroiled in endless struggles over budgets, facilities, and programs. I have heard senior pastors share how, if they had it to do over again, they would not have a school associated with their church.

This is because the ministry of the Christian school is not considered to be "church." You will recall from chapter 10 that *church* has become narrowly defined as those activities that take place on Sunday, Wednesday night, and during special events scheduled periodically throughout the year. When churches do not *expand their ministries* to include the weekday education ministry (regardless of the grade or age level) and only *attach* a school to the *church*, there will always be competition and conflict between the two entities.

When a church *expands its ministry* to include weekday education (a Christian school), it must develop a consistent theology of ministry for the entire church. This will mean that the families ministered to by the school are as much a part of the church as those ministered to in a Sunday morning worship service.

There is a strong tendency to deal with the school ministry in a totally different way than another "Sunday" ministry is treated. An example of this can be seen in the use of facilities. A church leader recently shared that it looked as if they were holding church in a school rather than the other way around—which would be the right way. I responded that if the school was the church ministering to families throughout the week, then it was the "church" holding "church" in the "church" regardless of what was on the walls in a room. The room decorations didn't define what was and what was not "church."

Other examples of this dichotomous way of looking at Christian school ministry and church ministry is seen when churches contemplate starting a school ministry. Some will argue that a school ministry shouldn't be started because only a small percentage of the families would be involved in it. Or the argument would be made that the market should drive whether or not a school ministry is started. However, this would not be the case if the church were considering starting an evangelism program. The church would start it because it is biblical to do so, regardless of the fact that a small percentage of the congregation would participate or that the community (the market) was not calling the church to have someone come and witness to them.

I have also seen a school ministry treated differently when it comes to finances. Church members will say that there should be no funds from the tithes and offerings of the church go to help fund the school ministry. They say that only those who actually use the school should totally fund its costs. However, they would not follow this same theology of ministry when it comes to the use of the family life center. There would be an outcry in the church if those families who used the life center were given a monthly bill according to their use of it. Church leaders and members must break out of the box that defines the church and the Christian school as separate entities.

On the other hand, many Christian schools are not supporting the local church as they should. School leaders do not see pastors supporting their schools and they, in turn, are not supportive of the church. Schools continue to expand their programs and activities with little, if any, consideration for what is happening in their community's churches. When school leaders try to get pastors involved in their schools through such activities as pastors' lunches or open houses, very few church leaders take the time to attend.

Conflicts also arise over the students of Christian schools in some local churches. Many of these students have a thorough knowledge of God's Word and are not challenged in their Sunday School classes or youth meetings. Sometimes the students may be better versed in the Bible than the church's lay teachers. This leads to situations where Christian school students tend to develop their own little groups and are looked upon as not being involved in the church's program. It is all too common to see Christian school students be unconcerned and uninvolved in the efforts of a church youth program aimed at evangelizing other teens in their community.

What are the solutions to these problems? How should the school relate to the church? The answers to these questions are found in the concept of kingdom education. Leaders in both the school and the church must realize that kingdom education principles transcend their own individual programs and plans. God wants to see Christians at home, church and school focus on fully preparing the next generation to capture the world for Christ. There is no time for Christian leaders to be arguing and debating over budgets, facilities, and programs. We must come to grips with the reality that it will take a concerted effort by the school and the church to properly educate the next generation.

Schools must never attempt to replace the church in a young person's life. If schools are involved in kingdom education, one of their primary goals should be to strengthen the local churches in their community. When I talk with Christian school administrators, I am often amazed at how many different churches are represented in the school's student population. When I served as superintendent for Lynchburg Christian Academy in Virginia, we conducted a survey and found that over 80 churches had students attending our school. This gave us a tremendous opportunity and responsibility to help strengthen many churches besides our own through our efforts at the Academy.

I believe that schools need to stress to their students the importance of individual involvement of believers in the local church. It must begin through personal example. By this, I mean that Christian school administrators and teachers must be actively involved in a local church. Schools must develop programs for students which teach the *importance* of the church and which encourage their *involvement* in their church. When the school properly educates students according to kingdom principles of education, the church has a high priority in everyone's life.

For my doctoral dissertation, I studied the religious beliefs and practices of Christian school graduates. These graduates had been out of school for 5 and 10 years. Even though the results showed that the longer the student attended a Christian school, the more active he or she was in the local church, the overall results were somewhat discouraging. Graduates who had attended Christian schools for eight or more years were twice as likely to hold a position in a local church than those who had attended fewer than eight years. However, church involvement was limited primarily to morning worship services and Sunday School classes.[2]

Of course, this is a growing problem in most Christian's lives today. Kingdom education will cause schools to develop stronger ties with local churches and to promote the practice of both staff members and students actively fulfilling their roles as members of the body of Christ.

Paul Young, former president of the Southern Baptist Educational Center, Olive Branch, Mississippi, wrote an article entitled, "The Marriage of the Church and Christian School: Why Do They Struggle?" Young provided some keen insight into how the school must relate to the church if kingdom education is to take place, pointing out that both the church and the school must understand the biblical philosophy of true education. That is what this book, *Kingdom Education,* is all about. Christian schools must be distinctively Christian. He addressed five basic questions to school leaders:

1. Is my school more concerned about knowledge (academic facts) than wisdom (knowing God's ways)?
2. Is my school more concerned with developing technical competencies than developing godly character?
3. Does my school plan more than it prays?
4. Does my school emphasize school rules more than scriptural principles?
5. Is my school curriculum-centered rather than teacher-centered? [3]

When schools can answer these questions from God's perspective, they will find themselves poised to develop a strong relationship with the church. When kingdom principles of education are the driving forces within both the school and the church, exciting things begin to happen. Many philosophical and logistical problems are resolved when the school and the church are committed to doing things God's way.

Kingdom education requires a three-strand cord to link the home, the school and the church. Solomon made it clear that a single strand can be easily broken, while two strands together are stronger. However, three strands of cord cannot easily be broken. The school must see its role as one of support—first for the home and then for the church. The school must never see itself as being more important than the church—that philosophy is completely contrary to God's Word. However, when the school and church are properly related to one another, kingdom education becomes effective.

Dr. Derek Keenan summed up this in a recent article when he stated, "a strong school-church relationship is a wonderful opportunity for young people to see the Body of Christ, with its diversity of gifts and personalities, functioning together." [4]

13

THE SCHOOL AND THE BIBLE

The Bible is indeed among books,
what the diamond is among precious stones.[1]
Robert Boyle

Dr. Al Mohler, President of Southern Seminary, recently stated, "Christian education that is not driven by the centrality of Scriptures is 'a lie!'"[2] I believe we can go one step further and state that *education without the Bible is a myth!* God's Word is the foundation for all knowledge. Christ said that God's Word would never fade away. It is everlasting. The Bible is our source of truth.

Kingdom education is founded on the Word of God. True education must, therefore, be Bible-based. If a school is going to support the home in providing kingdom education for its children, it must be committed to this reality. When the Bible is removed from the classroom, kingdom education cannot take place. Unfortunately, this has already happened in most state-run schools all around the world. In an effort to cater to the demands of pluralism, the United States has followed suit and, for all intents and purposes, has removed the Bible from public instruction. This reality, coupled with the teaching of evolution as scientific fact, has caused education to become secular in nature.

John Piper has captured the result of a purely secular education: "With the wave of an imaginary wand, the Darwinists sweep God out of heaven and Christ off the earth. Then they go to the classrooms of the nation and say, 'Respect each other and do good'—and wonder why kids kill each other like animals."[3] In the 1950s Gaebelein noted: "Our culture has lost its way because God and the Bible ... have been removed from influence in our schools. The authority of the transcendent God of the universe has been replaced by a society who worships at the feet of man and his accomplishments." [4]

In light of the present condition of secular education, it is amazing to study how the Founding Fathers of the United States viewed God's Word and education. Benjamin Rush was one of the most prolific writers of this group of distinguished men. On numerous occasions he boldly proclaimed that the Bible is an essential ingredient to true education. Consider his thoughts on what would happen if God's Word were to be removed from the classroom. "In contemplating the political institutions of the United States, [if we were to remove the Bible from schools] I lament that we waste so much time and money in punishing crimes and take so little pains to prevent them. We profess to be republicans, and yet we neglect the only means of establishing and perpetuating our republican forms of government, that is, the universal education of our youth in the principles of Christianity by means of the Bible."[5]

We have witnessed Rush's prediction coming true. We are a country that spends its time and money on *punishing* crime rather than *preventing* crime. Rush also believed: "No man was ever early instructed in the truths of the Bible without having been made wiser or better by the early operation of these impressions upon his mind."[6] He saw that the Bible was critical to man's salvation and that salvation was dealt a blow when the Bible was removed from the classroom in other countries. "The great enemy of the salvation of man, in my opinion, never invented a more effectual means of removing Christianity from the world than by persuading mankind that it was improper to read the Bible in schools."[7]

Fisher Ames was a member of the first Congress, and he proposed the wording for the First Amendment of our Constitution. He understood that this amendment did not separate religion from government. As Ames saw the addition of new schoolbooks into the classroom, he was concerned that this would lead to a de-emphasis of the Bible in the children's lessons. In 1809 he stated these concerns: "Why then, if these books for children must be retained, as they should, should not the Bible regain the place it once held as a school book? Its morals are pure, its examples, captivating and noble; the reverence of the sacred book that is thus early impressed lasts long, and probably not impressed in infancy, never takes firm hold of the mind."[8]

Noah Webster was another American statesman who recognized the important role that the Bible is to play in the educational process. He expressed concern that if the Bible were treated as a mere school textbook, it would become trivialized. "Will not a familiarity, contracted by a careless disrespectful reading of the sacred volume, weaken the influence of its precepts upon the heart? ... My wish is not to see the Bible excluded from schools but to see it used as a system of religion and morality".[9]

Thousands of Christian schools have been established in this country over the past four decades. They continue to grow both in number and enrollment. There have also been a great many families turning to home education over the last couple of decades. These two movements have been driven primarily by the effects of a secular educational system void of truth. However, it is imperative that both Christian schools and home-school families make certain that God's Word remains the *cornerstone* of their educational efforts, or else they will experience the same demise as most secular schools.

There are signs of an effort to limit use of the Bible to the Bible class-room and chapel and out of the academic disciplines. As this happens, the school is beginning its slide away from true kingdom education. Dr. Frank Spina, President of Seattle Pacific University, recently stated in an article entitled, "What Makes It Christian?" that, "a Christian school is Christian if, and only if, Christian content is central to the whole undertaking. Every subject of study is to be seen from the perspective of Christianity."[10]

Greene reminds us that "it brings no honor to the Holy Spirit if we then proceed to treat the ordinary school studies, which are derived totally from the created world, as if they had nothing to do with God. They are laden with meaning because they are all part of God's way of giving Himself to us, of making Himself known to us. ... The Word of God is the unifying element in all of reality."[11]

God's Word must remain the controlling point of all instruction if we are going to stay within God's plan for educating future generations. To do otherwise is to turn kingdom education into another myth. How does the school establish the Bible as the foundation of all instruction? It begins with the school leaders—the board members, administration, and faculty. School leaders must make the Bible the primary residence of their personal study. By this, I mean that we need to be spending more time in God's Word than in man's books and texts.

Picture yourself going outside on a bright sunny day. To battle the harshness of the bright sunshine, you might put on a pair of sunglasses. If you were to put on a pair that had green-tinted lenses, you would quickly discover that everything took on a green tint. The same would be true if you were to wear glasses with brown lenses. Everything, regardless of its true color, would be tinted by the color of the sunglasses.

God's Word should be our sunglasses in life. Kingdom educators must make certain they put on the glasses of the Bible every time they study the subject(s) they will teach to their students. By doing this, every subject will be colored by God's Word. The teacher will see the subject matter from God's perspective rather than man's. This will allow the teacher to recognize truth from error when preparing to teach his or her students. This is because truth is "a Person, Jesus Christ, who is pleased to reveal God to us through the various sides of the creation. ... We must avoid the impression that academics represent the fullness of what school is all about. Knowing God in and through the creation is what is important."[12]

There is a drive for academic excellence throughout the educational arena today. Everyone is striving to excel in knowledge. However, knowledge without the intelligence of God's Word can never become wisdom. God's Word is the only integrating factor that can bring true meaning to any subject and, therefore, true meaning for life.

I owe a great deal to Dr. Roy Lowrie, Jr. He mentored many of my generation in Christian school education. His entire life was dedicated to instilling the importance of a Bible-based education in the lives of future generations. Dr. Lowrie used an illustration that has stuck in my mind from the first time I saw it until this very day. He would hold up a book in one hand and God's Word in the other hand. The first book would represent any book written by man. Then Dr. Lowrie would state that there are only three ways that man's book and God's book can be used together.

The first way was to look at the Bible through the writings of man. As one did this, whatever contradictions that arose between the two books would be considered in the light of man's book. This means that if something in the Bible contradicted what man wrote, that portion of the Bible would be considered in error and would be discarded. This is because man's book was being used as the filter to interpret and critique God's Word. For example, if something in the Bible contradicted what was being taught in the science classroom, the Bible must be wrong and the science textbook would be considered truthful.

The second way that the Bible and God's Word are compared to each other is by holding them up side by side. Here, one considers what is written in both books and the reader determines which one contains truth and which one contains error. The individual can pick and choose from both books and determine what is true and what should be taught. In both of these first two scenarios, there is one commonality. Man is determining what is true and what is not.

The final way that man's books and God's Word can be used together is by viewing man's works through God's Word. Here, the Bible becomes the filter by which error is defined and truth is revealed. If Christians really believe that the Bible is the inerrant, infallible, and eternal Word of God, then they must also believe that it must be used to scrutinize any subject being studied. If God's Word does not find its place in education as the unifying factor of all instruction, then we are saying that man's books are more reliable than God's Book.

Regardless of the name that is on any school entrance, kingdom education only takes place where God's Word is central to all instruction. It only takes place where the teachers think and act from a biblical worldview, and this can happen *only* when the teacher studies the Word as much as he or she studies the subject being taught. Kingdom education demands that God's Word be the integrating factor between faith and learning. The school must have this relationship with the Bible; otherwise education from God's perspective cannot take place.

In this section, we have discovered that the school is to support the biblical beliefs and values that are to be taught in a Christian home. As the home and school join together, they are to instill within the hearts and minds of children the importance of the church in God's kingdom. Finally, we see how God's Word must undergird every subject taught at home, church and school for true education to take place.

Kingdom education defines God's plan for educating future generations. For this to take place, Christians must make some critical decisions concerning the school their children will attend to adequately prepare the next generation for the future.

Section V

KINGDOM EDUCATION:
THE FUTURE

14

THE DANGER OF DUALISM

God's plan for the advancement of His kingdom depends on His relationship to His people.[1]
Henry Blackaby

By now I trust that you have been challenged to give greater attention to the principles of kingdom education as God has set forth in His Word. My prayer is that you have become convinced that the home, the church, and the school must be playing off the same page if our children are going to be trained *in the nurture and admonition of the Lord.* As you and I prepare for the future, we must be aware of a subtle danger that can destroy any desire we might have to be involved in kingdom education. Albert Greene refers to this danger as *dualism*.[2]

Dualism is an effort to divide life into different parts and operate each part from a different worldview perspective. In other words, we actually live our lives in such a way that part of our day is run from a man-centered worldview and other parts of our day are operated from a God-centered worldview. Patrick Morley identifies this effort to merge two or more belief systems into one as *syncretism.* He explains that it is an effort "to have the best of the Christian life view and the best of a humanistic life view at the same time. It is to worship Christ, but not give up our idol."[3] Throughout the Old Testament God warned the nation of Israel not to mingle with other nations. This warning was given so that God's people would not "intermarry with the culture"[4] and live dualistic or syncretistic lives. God knows that when this occurs, it will result in people becoming cultural Christians and their hearts will be turned to other gods. Once, as I tried to get this point across to a group of Christian adults, I had them play a word game with me. I would say a word and they would have to guess what word I was thinking of. I began by saying the word *hot*. Soon, someone said the word *cold*. I told them that response was correct.

I then said the word *up* The entire group responded by saying, *down*. Again, I said that was correct. Next I said the word *in*. In quick unison, they replied *out*. Once again, they had answered correctly. Then came the test. I said the word *secular*. The group, in unison, shouted *sacred*. They had proved my point. Far too many Christians live their lives as if they can be divided into two contrasting lifestyles.

Too often we believe that there is a secular part of life and a sacred or spiritual part of life. That is why so many Christians appear to have life so right on Sunday, only to have it fall apart on Monday morning! When one believes there are two sides of life, a secular side and a spiritual side, he has succumbed to dualism. The result is devastating. Dualism forces life into a series of unrelated compartments. A person tries to find meaning and purpose in life but cannot discover it because there is no unifying factor. He becomes frustrated because he isn't able to live a vibrant Christian life. He justifies his lack of abundant life by saying that society has changed and the dynamic, vibrant Christian is no longer possible.

The greater danger is the tendency to believe that education also can be divided into the spiritual and the secular. This is what Horace Mann paraphrased when he said, "Let the home and church teach faith and values and the school teach facts."[5] The logical next step is to believe that math, science, history, and language arts are only secular subjects, while the Bible is only a religious subject. It follows then, that we become very careful to make sure that we allow only Christian teachers to instill the truths of the Bible into the minds and hearts of our children. However, anyone who knows the facts of math, or science, or history, or any other subject is best qualified to teach these subjects to our children. This logic is fatally flawed.

The truth of the matter is that we cannot separate beliefs and values from any area of knowledge. This means that the beliefs and values of the teacher will be closely attached to any subject matter which that person presents to students. When we hold to the belief that certain subjects are secular in nature, we are apt to disregard the beliefs held by the teacher who will be influencing the hearts and minds of our children. In reality, we are saying that anyone, even an unsaved individual, can explain life here on earth to our children. How can we forget that this world is God's and only He can explain its origin, its present condition, and its future end? I agree with the words of Walter Ediger who said, "It is impossible to separate God's world from God. How then, is it possible to teach about God's world and leave Him out?"[6] Greene puts it this way, "Since all 'facts' are created and since the living God would not make something that is meaningless, … there is no basis for separating facts from values."[7]

Allowing secular thought to influence the education of our children will lead them to see life as compartmentalized, where God is relevant in some areas but irrelevant in other areas. Consider the words of Dr. A. A. Hodge of Princeton Seminary:

> If every party in the state has the right of excluding from public schools whatever he does not believe to be true, then he that believes most must give way to him that believes least, and he that believes least must give way to him that believes absolutely nothing, no matter in how small a minority the atheists and agnostics may be.
>
> I am as sure as I am of the fact of Christ's reign that a comprehensive and centralized system of national education, *separated from religion*, as is now commonly proposed, will prove the most appalling enginery for the propagation of anti-Christian and atheistic unbelief and of anti-social nihilistic ethics, social and political, which this sin-rent world has ever seen.[8]

Dr. B. H. Bode also saw the destructive nature of a dualistic philosophy of education when he wrote these words in 1948.

> The time came when this beautiful harmony (between education and theology) was disrupted. When the schools had to take account of the advance in knowledge and the changes in our material and social environment, the continuity between tradition and education gave way to controversy and conflicts and the eventuality brought on the present situation. Mechanistic physics became a challenge to supernaturalism; evolution

undertook to replace the account in Genesis; psychology rejected the traditional doctrine of the soul; economics became a threat to historic property rights. There was no longer a common foundation for moral judgment.[9]

How do Christians avoid dualism? The answer is found in our relationship to Jesus Christ. Let me explain it this way. When I received Jesus as my Lord and Savior, I entered into a personal love relationship with Him. Jesus wants that love relationship to be personal, intimate and the controlling factor in all of my life. When my love relationship does not control my entire life, the relationship deteriorates.

The analogy of marriage sheds some important light on the importance of this concept. Men, can you remember your wedding day? Your beautiful wife-to-be came down that aisle, and together you stood before the pastor. The pastor asked you some questions. You said, "I do." She said, "You'd better!" After the wedding, you probably went on a honeymoon and shared some wonderful days together before coming back home and going back to work.

Suppose that on Monday morning, you kiss your new bride good-bye, tell her you love her and head off to work. On your morning break you call her and tell her you miss her. You repeat this during lunch and then again on your afternoon break. However, when 4:00 p.m. comes and work is finished, you don't rush home or even call your wife. Instead, you go out with your buddies. You have some pizza, go bowling and then watch Monday night football at one of their homes.

When the game is over and it is almost midnight, you say goodnight and head home. You turn the key in the lock and walk into your home to find your wife pacing the floor. She has a very worried look on her face and asks, "Where have you been? What happened? I have been worried that you were hurt or in an accident. I have called the police and hospitals." You glibly reply, "Oh, I was out with the guys tonight."

Her worried look suddenly turns to one of anger. Even though divorce is not considered an option, murder may be justified. She exclaims, "You were out with the guys? You didn't even let me know! Why didn't you call? I am your wife; we're married. I can't believe you were so thoughtless."

Then you say, "I know I am married, but not on Monday nights from 4:00 p.m. to midnight."

By now you are thinking, what a stupid concept! If I approached my marriage relationship with my wife in that way, the marriage would soon be in shambles. It is the same way between a parent and a child. When that newborn child comes home from the hospital, we become full-time parents. We can't tell the little one, "I am your parent, but not from midnight to 6:00 a.m." If your experience was like mine, your little baby quickly let you know that his relationship with you was going to impact every part of your life—even at 2:00 a.m.

All of us would be quick to say that marriage and parenting cannot be divided into times of being married (or not) or being a parent (or not). No, the marriage relationship and the child-parent relationship must impact every aspect of life or the relationships will disintegrate. If this is true for mere human relationships, why do most Christians think that they can act otherwise in regard to their relationship with Jesus Christ? Why do we believe that we can divide life into the secular and the spiritual, and by doing this, act as if we are not Christians when living in the secular?

Henry Blackaby, in his hallmark work, *Experiencing God*, points out that "a love relationship with God is more important than any other single factor in your life. ... Everything in your Christian life, everything about knowing Him and experiencing Him, everything about knowing His will, depends on the quality of your love relationship to God."[10] Since this love relationship is the most important part of God's plan for the advancement of His kingdom, then it must control all aspects of life—including the area of education.

Dualism would have us believe that anyone can teach our children and it won't impact their view of God. Kingdom education says just the opposite. It demands that we view everything, including education, from an eternal perspective. Parents and church leaders must be able to recognize dualism, and then do everything possible to drive it far from their lives and the lives of their children.

If kingdom education is to be effective in our families, then dualistic thinking must be avoided like the plague. Colson drives this reality home with conviction.

What's clear ... from creation onward, is that God's rule
extends to everything. From our bank accounts to our business dealings to our *educational curriculum* to our social justice
issues to our environmental concerns to our political choices in
the voting booth—everything must reflect the fact that God's
righteous rule extends to all of life. ... In obedience to this
mandate, we must affirm that truth involves all of life and then
define and teach a Christian world-view.[11]

Even though many Christians attempt to divide life into the secular
and the sacred compartments, it is actually impossible to separate Christianity [one's relationship with Christ] from any part of life. In reality when
we attempt to do this, "some aspect of the creation becomes supreme in
education and life instead of the living God. ... All humans, if they do not
serve God in Christ, are addicted to something in the
creation."[12]

Once every area of our lives is being directed by a Bible-based worldview perspective, we will be able to follow God's plan for educating future
generations.

15

RENEWING THE MIND

There is no longer a Christian mind. As a thinking being, the modern Christian has succumbed to secularization.[1]
Harry Blarmires

In his book *The Christian Mind: How Should a Christian Think?* Harry Blarmires notes that "a prime mark of the Christian mind is that it cultivates the eternal perspective. That is to say, it looks beyond this life to another one. It is supernaturally orientated, and brings to bear upon earthly considerations the fact of Heaven and the fact of Hell."[2] Blarmires' statement reminds us that education is really a spiritual battle. It is a battle for the minds and the hearts of our children. There are many forces at work waging war against our children's minds. The world, the flesh, and the devil all want to control their hearts, and each entity knows that this is accomplished by controlling their minds. Someone has well said,

> Sow a thought, reap an act. Sow an act, reap a habit.
> Sow a habit, reap a character. Sow a character, reap a destiny!

This spiritual battle is of extreme importance. However, there is something that Christian adults must do before we can adequately understand how to mold the minds and the hearts of our children. We must obey God's command found in Romans 12:2, where Paul wrote that the Christian must "not be conformed to this world, but be transformed by the *renewing of your mind*" (NKJV, emphasis mine). Even though most Christians know this passage, few understand its full meaning. Throughout this book we have seen that the average Christian today is not thinking biblically. This is why Guinness claims that most Christians are "cultural imitators and adapters rather than originators." 3

We hear all the time that the vast majority of Americans believe in God. Some studies show that one out of every three adults indicate that they are "born again." Patrick Morley asks the questions, "Where are they? And why hasn't their faith turned the world upside down?" His answer points out the reality that most Christians don't think biblically and therefore don't act any different from this world. He states that "many of us have so adroitly melded Christianity into our culture that we are completely camouflaged; no one can tell we are there." 4

I was on a plane from Nashville to Atlanta with a former pastor of mine. During our discussion, I made the statement that I thought that 75 percent of the adult members of his church had probably never gone through a deliberate process of renewing their minds. He was quiet for a time and then responded, "Glen, I think you are wrong. It may be more like 85-90 percent!" I would remind you of Barna's conclusions, based on 10 years of research, that caused him to state that only 7 or 8 percent of today's Christians have a biblical understanding.5 The church today may not be thinking or acting from a biblical perspective for the first time in our nation's history.

We can never attempt to fulfill the mandate of kingdom education for the next generation if we do not give careful attention to God's command to renew our own minds. This must take place if we are going to think and act biblically. Guinness says it well when he challenges every Christian to think "about anything and everything in a consistently Christian way— in a manner that is *shaped, directed,* and *restrained* by the truth of God's Word and God's Spirit" (emphasis mine).6 Then, and only then, will we be able to understand God's plan for educating future generations. In order to have a true understanding of what it takes to renew one's mind, consider Paul's exhortation to the church at Corinth.

> *For though we walk in the flesh, we do not* war *according to the flesh. For the* weapons *of our* warfare *are not carnal but mighty in God for pulling down strongholds, casting down arguments and every high thing that exalts itself against the knowledge of God,* bringing every thought into captivity to the obedience of Christ (2 Cor. 10:3-5, NKJV, emphasis mine).

Chuck Swindoll, in his book *Living Above the Level of Mediocrity*, gives a vivid illustration of this important passage. He explains how, in ancient times, people would build walls around a city for protection. At important junctures in the wall, they would build tall towers to provide strategic locations from which an advancing enemy could be seen. When a city was under attack, military strategists would be assigned to these towers to direct the city's defense against the enemy. Anyone who wanted to capture the city knew that the important thing was to capture the military strategists and render the city defenseless.[7]

Renewing one's mind is described by Paul as a spiritual battle. In this battle, we must, by God's power, scale the walls (strongholds of tradition) of our minds, ascend the towers (human arguments), and capture each and every thought (military strategists) of our minds. It is our thoughts that must be taken captive to Christ or God's Word. In other words, we must take all of our thoughts about every aspect of life and allow them to be scrutinized by the keen eye of God's Word. When our thoughts and ideas do not line up with Scripture, these thoughts must be recognized as disobedient and cast out of our minds immediately.

A unique picture of this type of spiritual warfare is found in Nehemiah. You will recall that Nehemiah is the account of how one man was used by God to rebuild the walls around the city of Jerusalem. It is often studied as a book of the Bible that can provide us with insights into good leadership and how to handle opposition in doing God's will. However, I have come to see how this book is also an allegory of how one is to build a godly life. In Nehemiah 13:4 we find two characters involved a unique relationship:

> *Before this, Eliashib the priest, having authority over the store-rooms of the house of God, was allied with Tobiah. And he had prepared for him a large room, where previously they had stored the grain offerings, the frankincense, the articles, the tithes of grain, the new wine and oil (NKJV).*

At first this relationship seems quite innocent, but when we consider who Eliashib and Tobiah were, we get a much different picture. Eliashib was a high priest. He and his fellow priests helped rebuild the walls. In fact, in chapter 3:1 you will find that these men set the Sheep Gate in place. Tobiah was one of Nehemiah's tormentors. He was the one who mocked what God's people were doing and predicted that the wall would fall apart if even a little fox would run up on it. He was constantly opposing God's work in Jerusalem. He even was involved in schemes to distract and harm Nehemiah.

Do you realize the irony of this situation? The walls around Jerusalem had now been rebuilt. The city was safe and well. However, when everything looked perfect, there was a major problem. In the temple area, there was a small room. The priest had authority over this room and was supposed to keep it stocked with sacred articles that were used for worshipping God. Instead of using his authority properly, Eliashib allowed wicked Tobiah to move into this room with all his worldly goods.

This is a very accurate picture of the situation many Christians find themselves in today. They are saved and from the outside everything looks fine. They attend church, read their Bibles occasionally, and may even give regularly to the church. All the walls of defense seem to be in place. However, something both deceptive and dangerous is taking place. In the center of their lives is a small room over which they have authority. God desires that they store sacred things in this room, things that can be used to worship their Lord and Savior. However, like Eliashib, they have given the room over to wicked Tobiah and his worldly goods.

You are probably asking, "What room is he talking about?" *This room is our mind.* We have each been given authority over our mind. We are instructed to guard it and renew it so that we will think and act from a biblical perspective. Yet, too many of us allow Tobiah to dwell in comfort in the room meant to store God's thoughts. We think that everything is fine because we hear good messages in church, read our Bibles and pray once in awhile to God. Isn't that enough to renew my mind? The answer is a resounding *NO!* Renewing the mind is warfare. It takes more than merely reading and listening to things about God. We must go on the attack and start taking our thoughts, acts, habits, and characters captive to Christ.

Look at the drastic action Nehemiah took when he realized what Eliashib had done:

> *I came to Jerusalem and discovered the evil that Eliashib had done for Tobiah, in preparing a room for him in the courts of the house of God. And it grieved me bitterly; therefore I threw all the household goods of Tobiah out of the room. Then I commanded them to cleanse the rooms; and I brought back into them the articles of the house of God (Neh. 13:7, NKJV).*

Nehemiah did not take this lying down. He saw Eliashib's actions as war, and he followed specific steps to correct this destructive situation.

1. He grieved bitterly over the situation.
2. He threw all of Tobiah's goods out of the room.
3. He cleansed the room completely.
4. Finally, he replaced Tobiah's goods with those of God.

This is the same type of action you and I must take on a regular basis. When we recognize that this world's thoughts are in our minds, we need to be grieved bitterly over this dangerous and destructive condition. Then we must throw those thoughts out and cleanse our minds through confession to Christ. Finally, we must put God's thoughts in our minds so that we can know Him and understand His purposes and ways.

Some of you may be thinking that this really doesn't apply to you. After all, you have been a Christian for over 20 years or more. However, what we fail to understand is that we were all born in sin. Tobiah's thoughts were part of this sin nature. Unless we have gone through an evaluation process concerning all of our beliefs and values as I have just described, we have not renewed our minds. In my own experience, this is a never-ending battle. We must remember that "only a *reformation* of our belief system will give us the competence to bring the life-changing knowledge of God back into our culture and society"[8] and enable us to raise a godly generation in Christ.

Kingdom education demands that Christians have the mind of Christ, not only present but in control of our lives. This can only take place when we arm ourselves for battle, scrutinize all of our thoughts, and bring them under the captivity of the truth of God's Word. Paul warned the Colossian Christians that they were to "beware lest anyone cheat you through philosophy and empty deceit, according to the tradition of men, according to the basic principles of the world, and not according to Christ" (Colossians 2:8, NKJV). How do you view the education of the next generation? Is it according to the traditions of our society? Is it according to the basic principles of this world? Or is it according to Christ and His Word? The answers to these questions will determine if we are ready to follow God's plan for educating future generations.

16

A CALL
TO ACTION

*Today's educators are like the field general who has become
so involved in the problems and tactics of the immediate battle
that he neglects the overall strategy of the war,
and may even have forgotten why it is being fought.*[1]
Philip May

The Christian home, the church, and the school have neglected the over-all strategy of the war for the minds and hearts of our children for too long a time. Some may have even forgotten why it is being fought. I have shared with you lessons that God has taught me over the years concerning the education of future generations. The more I search the Scriptures, the more I realize the importance of understanding and following the kingdom principles of education that have been presented in this book.

The move away from these principles has occurred at a slow pace over a long period of time. However, the move toward a total secularization of education and society is advancing at an alarming speed today. In fact, Nord has accurately stated that "the great majority of Americans also lead largely secular lives and think about the world in largely secular terms. ... We have privatized our religion as we have secularized our culture."[2] It is time that Christians give immediate attention to what God has to say about how our children must be educated. I want to go back to the instruction from God to His people in Deuteronomy 6. I have a deep conviction that Christian adults must, once again, focus on God and begin loving Him with all of our heart, soul and strength. This is the only way that we will find ourselves able to hear from God and get clear direction concerning kingdom education.

Parents must once again take full responsibility for the proper education of their children. It is not a responsibility of the government or the church. It is our assignment, as parents, from God, Himself. I challenge every parent reading this book to go back and reread Section II. Ask God to lay upon your heart what He specifically wants you to do concerning the education of your children. Make sure that you do not waste energy and resources in giving your children things which are temporal or things which they do not need, while failing to give them the things that are eternal and most important to life.

Pastors and church leaders must carefully study these compelling principles of kingdom education. Diligent effort must be given to instruct the parents of our churches in these principles. Instruction must come from the pulpit, the Sunday School classroom, and the Discipleship Training meetings. Second only to evangelism, kingdom education needs to be the most important aspect of the church's ministry. Without proper training, our children will never be able to fulfill the Great Commission when they assume the adult leadership of the church.

Some churches will find that God wants them to expand their ministry to include schooling. Others will not find this to be God's will. Regardless of whether or not God leads a church to have such a ministry, every church needs to make an all-out effort to support schooling that is true to the principles of kingdom education. This support is not an option but an obligation to God and the future of His church.

The *Baptist Faith and Message,* a statement adopted by the Southern Baptist Convention in 1925 and revised in 1963, places importance on supporting Christian schools:

> The cause of education in the Kingdom of Christ is co-ordinate with the causes of missions and general benevolence, and should receive along with these the liberal support of the churches. An adequate system of Christian schools is necessary to a complete spiritual program for Christ's people.[3]

The statement gives clear indication that the term *Christian schools* did not merely apply to higher education when it refers to "a teacher in a

Christian school, college, or seminary."[4] The SBC revised and expanded this statement in 2000:

> Christianity is the faith of enlightenment and intelligence. In Jesus Christ abide all the treasures of wisdom and knowledge. All sound learning is, therefore, a part of our Christian heritage. The new birth opens all human faculties and creates a thirst for knowledge. Moreover, the cause of education in the Kingdom of Christ is co-ordinate with the causes of missions and general benevolence, and should receive along with these the liberal support of the churches. An *adequate system of Christian education* is necessary to a complete spiritual program for Christ's people (emphasis mine).[5]

The church must heed this call for an *adequate system of Christian education* as being *necessary to a complete spiritual program for Christ's people.* It clearly points out that the home, church, and school must be united under a common set of biblical principles that will drive every aspect of our children's education. This doctrinal statement sets an example that I pray all churches will take to heart. Throughout His Word, God makes it clear that the education of the next generation is close to His heart. Therefore, it should receive the *liberal* support of the churches.

Every church must support the Christ-centered, Bible-based education of its children. If a church does not operate such an educational ministry, then it should support those programs that serve its families. If this were to happen, I believe every Christian family could afford to send their children to a school that would value and reinforce the family's spiritual beliefs and follow kingdom education principles.

I realize that I am making bold statements with which many will struggle or oppose. Some may say that such ideas would offend those Christians who now teach and administrate in public schools within the community. Understand that I am not talking about *where* God places us as adults to be involved in spiritual battle. I am talking about where and how God wants our children to be trained so that they can be fully equipped to be salt and light in this world.

Churches must also recognize and reach out to those families in their congregations who choose to educate their children at home. Home schooling or home education is growing at a fast pace. These parents, for the most part, believe that the home is the best place for them to educate their child(ren) according to kingdom principles of education. These families need the support of their churches. Many churches are equipped and staffed in the area of media libraries, music departments, drama departments, and recreation departments. These programs, and others like them, provide tremendous opportunities for the church to minister, not only to their members but also to the community at large.

Many churches are currently operating a school ministry, and hundreds more are starting schools every year. Some important actions need to be taken by these ministries. First, these schools must be an integral part of the ministry of the church. The church and school must come together to impact the education of the children by sharing time, energy, space, calendar, staff, and resources. It is time to put an end to conflicts over space, calendar, and funding. The church should advance the cause of the school while the school advances the cause of the church—resulting in both parts of the ministry evangelizing the community.

Christian schools and home-school families must make every effort to maintain a Bible-based, Christ-centered philosophy undergirding every aspect of their educational programs. God's Word must be the foundation on which all teaching is established. Policies and procedures must reflect an all-out commitment to biblical principles. Kingdom-focused schools cannot give in to becoming institutions where a secular curriculum is merely Christianized by adding some Bible classes and chapel to the program.

I am convinced that academic excellence will be a key result when a school keeps Christ preeminent in all that it does. When a school focuses primarily on academic excellence and not on Christ, it usually compromises its biblical integrity and, therefore, cannot be academically excellent. This means that great care must be given to ensuring that the school does not simply try to be "as good as" some other institution.

Finally, kingdom education schools must put a greater focus on teaching their students the importance of the church. Coordinated efforts must be made to develop a heart for evangelism in the life of each student. Children and youth who receive a true kingdom education will see the necessity of being active members in a local church. They will want to make sure that all members of the body of Christ are functioning well. It is my personal conviction that future generations *must* receive a biblically-based education at home, church, and school if we are to see the kingdom of God advance throughout the world. A child that receives such an education will be best equipped to serve Christ in a meaningful way.

Recently, I was trying to put into words what is taking place in our society today concerning the shaping of our children's beliefs and values. An analogy suddenly captivated my thinking. I began writing down my thoughts and studying the analogy. The picture portrayed in my mind was what I have seen take place all across the country. Let me share that analogy with you. I ask that you consider its meaning carefully in light of what you have just read.

What's A Parent To Do?

Your four children are with friends for the entire evening. Every task at home is finished, and you and your wife have nothing else on your schedule. How will you take advantage of this one time when the children are gone and you are free for the night? You have read about a new theater that has recently opened in town. Since it was funded by the town, there is no admission being charged. The two of you decide to go to see what is playing at this theater.

Upon arriving, you discover that there are four movies being shown. Since admission is free, you are able to attend any one or all four shows. You decide to go into the first room and watch a film entitled *Tolerance*. This title sounds interesting; maybe it is a thought-provoking thriller. As the movie begins, you feel uneasy about a subtle theme that seems to be running throughout the plot. Just a short time into the film, this theme becomes clear. The movie is all about justifying and promoting homosexuality. Its message is blatant and glorifies homosexuality as just another alternate lifestyle that deserves the same respect as any other type of personal relationship. You know that God's Word says this is perversion and therefore, you and your wife quickly leave in disgust.

You look at the marquee and decide to go and see one of the other films entitled, *Safety Zone*. This film promises to be action-packed. No sooner do you sit down to enjoy this movie when you realize this, too, is glorifying what you remember as free love of the 60s. The film is even promoting this type of lifestyle for teenagers. The main message being shown on the screen and blared through the speakers is that it is altogether natural for young people to be sexually active. However the film points out that because of disease and possible pregnancy, it is vital that safety be the rule by which to guide a sexually active lifestyle. Again, you and your wife quickly leave the room.

Well, there are two more shows left. The room next to you is showing a film entitled, *The Inner Man*. This film is advertised as one that will bring a sense of satisfaction and positive self-esteem to every viewer. Feeling relieved, you settle in, to hopefully watch something that will bring meaning to life. The film has been produced with outstanding imagery—*but* all of a sudden you realize that there is a mystical new-age theme being pumped out into the audience. The theme is leading you to reach down inside and discover all the good that is hidden in you beneath the surface. You are being told that to discover self-fulfillment, you need to be in touch with your inner being and to take advantage of your own crystal mind. Quickly you get up and run out, knowing that this type of thinking goes contrary to all you believe as a Christian.

You decide to at least try the last movie. After all, its title is *Freedom*. Surely, this must be a better movie. What can be more important than maintaining one's freedom? You enter the darkened room hoping with all of your heart that this will be a movie that gives you some relaxation and enjoyment. To your disappointment, you see that this film asserts that man was not created by God but is a natural phenomenon of evolution closely related to other animals. It is soon apparent that the movie denies the existence of anything supernatural—especially God. The movie spews out a message that declares that there are no moral absolutes and that every individual must decide for himself what is right or wrong. Soon it is clear that everything and anything can be justified—from abortion to divorce to physician-assisted suicide. Even though human life is not valued in this movie, there is a great emphasis on how important the environment is and how we must protect such creatures as the whale, the horned owl and other wildlife. Totally frustrated, you leave the movie.

As you leave the theater, you remark to one another what a wasted night it has been. You also begin to discuss how dangerous these films are. The messages were at first subtle and then became quite blatant. You become concerned because you believe many others will be attracted to the theater. After all, the building is absolutely beautiful, the furnishings are first class and the technology was quite astounding. Best of all, the cost was free!

You are just about to walk out the door and you glance over at the refreshment area. To your amazement, you see your four children buying popcorn and soft drinks. You quickly walk over to them and ask what they are doing here and what movie each was watching. They tell you that all their friends go here regularly. Their companions are from church and from the neighborhood. It turns out that each child was watching a different movie. However, they were all excited about the one they were watching and were telling each other how they needed to see each one.

As parents, you are forced to make a decision. You know that each of these films is promoting a philosophy that goes against your convictions as a Christian. You want to do what is right, but there are so many circumstances that come into play. If you take them out of the theater, what will they do? You don't want them out merely roaming the streets. It seems to be quite safe inside this beautiful building. Most of the neighborhood children are here. And then there is the situation with their friends. You know your children need to learn how to be influencing their peers in a positive way, and you don't want to offend your children in front of their peers. So what's a parent to do?

A. Take them with you from the theater?
B. Let them stay, but be with them to discuss each film?
C. Let them stay with their friends but encourage them to think through the meaning of the films and have a good testimony while they are there?
D. Find an alternative activity that would support your Christian convictions and take them to this activity right away?

The above scenario may seem extremely far fetched to many Christian parents. Yet, this is not merely a hypothetical situation. In reality, this type of free theater can be found in most any community. They are located in big cities, sprawling suburbs, small towns, and even rural villages. They are funded by the government, beautifully built and filled with the finest furnishings and technology. These theaters are thought to be *free* by the majority of American families. In actuality, they are referred to as our public schools.

I say this because, in an effort to be religiously neutral, the Bible has been denied as being the source of absolute truth. This has brought about the reality that, to a great extent, God has been removed from the classroom. In Blackaby's work, *Experiencing God*, he makes the point that *"truth is a person—Jesus Christ."* Therefore, when truth (The Bible) is removed, Christ is removed.[6]

When the Bible and God are absent from education, a wide variety of values are taught. There is no question that the films, *Tolerance, Safety Zone, The Inner Man, and Freedom* are being played over and over again throughout the day for all children to watch. Consider the following:

Tolerance is being shown in the social studies department. Here, societal values have been incorporated into the curriculum. The terms "community" and "family" have been given new definitions by which society is to operate. The goal is to lead children out of their prejudices and into a new culture where there are no biases, even when dealing with something as perverse as homosexuality.

Safety Zone is seen in many health and life science classes. It very seldom mentions abstinence, but follows the false assumption that when sex education is completely open and discussed, those young people who desire to be sexually active will at least practice safe sex. In many schools, safety devices are fully explained and even distributed to those watching this film.

The Inner Man is found playing in a variety of subjects. Literature classes, guidance counseling and self-esteem activities all attempt to get the message across to students that they, alone, should be the ones to determine what is right and wrong. Students are deliberately involved in these films through writing journals, role playing, and the use of imaginary guides. Self-esteem programs begin in the early grades, sometimes as early as kindergarten.

Freedom is also being shown in many classrooms. It has its earliest showing in the science classroom but is also supported in other subject areas. *Freedom* begins with the premise that man was not supernaturally created but is the result of an evolutionary process. Since God does not exist in this film, man becomes autonomous and must make decisions based on moral relevancy.

When one first sees the names of these films, there doesn't seem to be any cause for alarm. The terms are much a part of most Christian's vocabulary. However, the hidden agendas that lie below the surface of any educational program that is not founded on kingdom principles will destroy not only the fabric of the family, but that of society.

I did not share this story to attack public schools. However, it is intended to show that secular educational programs teach values that go against God and His Word. It was meant to stress the importance of God's plan for educating our children and youth. Education impacts eternity, and that education, void of biblical truth, ceases to qualify as part of God's plan. In I Samuel 15, God gave Saul specific instructions on what He wanted him to do as king. Saul followed these instructions to a certain point. However, he finally adjusted God's instruction to fit the pressures of society and what he considered to be appropriate. God's reaction was swift and severe. Not only did Saul lose his kingdom, God told Saul that He was sorry that He had ever made Saul king.

God gives Christian parents specific instructions on how He wants us to train (educate) our children. He warns us about allowing empty philosophies to take us captive and tells us to consciously take every thought and make it obedient to Christ (God's Word). He also instructs us not to follow human traditions and wisdom.

The challenge that kingdom education presents to every parent, teacher and leader is this: *Am I obeying God's instructions about my responsibilities? If not, is God sorry that He ever made me a parent?*

Time is of the essence. Christians can no longer ignore the principles that God has set forth in His Word concerning education. If we are going to educate future generations that will be equipped to serve Christ in all areas of society, we must act immediately. It must be a combined effort by parents, church leaders, and school leaders. Each entity has an essential role to play.

CHRISTIAN PARENTS

Parents must take full responsibility for the education of their children. They must first make sure that what is taking place in the home is true to God's Word. Then, they must see to it that their family is actively involved in a strong Bible-believing local church. Finally, Christian parents must choose schools that will support kingdom principles of education.

THE CHURCH

Church leaders need to support the home by instilling the principles of kingdom education in the hearts and minds of their adult members. It is also critically important that all churches support educational efforts that are true to God's plan of educating future generations. This means that churches must seek God's direction as to how they can support their home-school families and the Christian schools that serve their membership.

THE SCHOOL

Whether it is taking place in the home or a Christian school, kingdom education must be based on the truth of God's Word and the reality of Jesus Christ. Schools must base all of their teaching on the Scriptures and must see as part of their mission the need to strengthen the church so that the Great Commission can be accomplished.

The school must support the biblical principles and values of a Christian home. A school, operated by the principles of kingdom education, completes the legs of the stool that supports every child's education.

KINGDOM EDUCATION—A REALITY

My time of service for God is passing quickly. As I attempt to "finish the race," I want to focus my attention on the next generation. It is my desire to see my children and grandchildren love the Lord with all their heart, soul, and strength. I trust this book has instilled this same desire in your heart.

It is my conviction that the home, church and school can produce godly offspring by following the principles of kingdom education. When this occurs, parents can realize the truth of III John 4, "I have no greater joy than to hear that my children walk in truth" (KJV).

EPILOGUE

Every Christian who has read this book must make some very important decisions. As one makes decisions about the biblical principles of education, he or she must realize that a decision is a commitment to all of the consequences of one's choice. There are few decisions of greater importance to parents than ones that deal with how we raise or educate our children.

Christians must understand the significant influence that education has on a person's life, a fact illustrated throughout human history. Recall (see chapter 3) the attempts by King Nebuchadnezzar, Hitler, the Soviet Union, and Fidel Castro to control the minds of the youth and erase former religious commitment. King Nebuchadnezzar wanted the Hebrew teens to undergo a thorough 3-year educational program so that Daniel and his friends would be fit to serve Babylon. His plan indicated the "thoroughness in the Babylonian attempt to erase from their minds all memory of former religious commitment."[1]

All secular educational programs have had and continue to have the same desired outcome—to erase from our children's minds all memory of former religious commitment. Hitler used education to help him rise to power in Germany. During travels in the former Soviet Union, I learned that education was a key element for developing future generations of Soviet citizens committed to living by a communist worldview.

Chuck Colson noted that at Fidel Castro's 75th birthday party in 2001, he was seen presenting a Cuban flag to the head of the Cuban Communist Youth Organization, which symbolized Castro's commitment to instilling a communist worldview in the mind of every Cuban child. "Castro knows that in order to keep his regime alive, he must pass the torch of communism to the next generation. He knows that if he fails to teach Cuba's children the communist worldview, his revolution will eventually die out."[2] Castro's revolution will die out soon after his own death if indeed he is not successful in this one endeavor. All of his energy and resources are focused on this task.

Colson challenges the church to be equally committed to instilling a biblical worldview in every child's mind before we leave this earth. If we are not successful in doing so, Christianity as we know it in our country will die out soon after our own deaths.

It has taken over 150 years of secular education for our culture to get to its current condition, so we are not going to be able to reverse this overnight. Greene understood this reality: "This is not a project of one Sunday or one month or one year. It will take years, and radical reawakenings, for it to begin to produce the impact on society that the witness of the church should be producing."[3] Even though this will take some time, Christians must begin *now!*

Once we start, we cannot afford to get discouraged when we face obstacles and opposition. I recall the account of Peter stepping out of the boat to go to Jesus. He was the only disciple who had the courage and the faith to step out of the boat at the Lord's command. However, once out of the boat, he started to focus on the wind and waves breaking at his feet. He stopped focusing on what Christ had told him to do. The result was that Peter started to sink. Jesus said to Peter, "You of little faith, why did you doubt?" (Matt. 14:31, HCSB).

This book has presented God's commands regarding the education of our children and youth. The decision you must make first is whether or not to step out of the boat. I pray that millions of Christians will have the faith of Peter and step out in obedience to Christ.

However, once out of the boat, you will be tempted to focus on the winds and the waves surrounding you. Some of these obstacles may even come from other Christians. My challenge to you is "Don't doubt, stay focused on Christ and His Word, and keep walking!"

I want to go back to Lorin's testimony and share her closing comments with you.

> One final word to the parents out there. Choosing a school which your child will attend is often a very difficult task. Every year when registration time approaches, critical questions are asked. Performances are evaluated. Pros and cons are weighed.

Each year as you prayerfully contemplate this crucial decision, may I encourage you to seek not what is good for your children, but what is best. Seek not what is important, but what is essential. Seek not glamour, but godliness. Seek not a place that gives your children opportunities to socialize; seek first that which gives your children opportunities for servanthood. Seek not to increase their fun; seek to increase their faith. Seek not tools to make them rich; seek first to give them tools to make them righteous. Parents, seek not what makes your kids happy; seek first what makes your kids holy. Seek ye first the kingdom of heaven and His righteousness, and then sit back and claim God's promise that every single thing your children need to fulfill God's perfect plan for their lives will be given unto them.[4]

The choice is yours. What you decide to do with the principles set forth in this book will be reflected in the way you live your life. Remember that our lives make a statement to the next generation about what is really important in life. According to John Piper, the real alternative to the secularizing effect of education will be realized when future generations see all those who teach them to be "great Christian thinkers who are great lovers of God with profound allegiance to the truth of God's Word and razor-sharp discernment of all the subtle idols of our age. . . . Our problem is that so few people have ever tasted great Christian [kingdom] education or seen great Christian thinking going on from a profoundly God-centered perspective in an atmosphere where students can feel that [their teachers] would gladly die for Jesus."[5]

Today's parents face the same challenge that all Christians have faced. Will our children accept our faith or will they *"blend invisibly into a world that considers the Bible irrelevant?"*[6]

> *It is my prayer that every believer take seriously the principles of kingdom education and become committed to God's plan for educating future generations. May God bless you as you step out of the boat in obedience to God's Word.*

To Be Educated

By Carolyn Caines, Supervisor
Columbia Heights Christian Academy • Longview, Washington

If I learn my ABCs, can read 600 words per minute, and can write with perfect penmanship,
but have not been shown how to communicate with the Designer of all language,
I have not been educated.

If I can deliver an eloquent speech and persuade you with my stunning logic,
but have not been instructed in God's wisdom,
I have not been educated.

If I have read Shakespeare and John Locke and can discuss their writings with keen insight,
but have not read the greatest of all books—the Bible—and have no knowledge
of its personal importance.
I have not been educated.

If I have memorized addition facts, multiplication tables, and chemical formulas,
but have never been disciplined to hide God's Word in my heart,
I have not been educated.

If I can explain the law of gravity and Einstein's theory of relativity,
but have never been instructed in the unchangeable laws of the One Who orders our universe,
I have not been educated.

If I can classify animals by their family, genus and species,
and can write a lengthy scientific paper that wins an award,
but have not been introduced to the Maker's purpose for all creation,
I have not been educated.

If I can recite the Gettysburg Address and the Preamble to the Constitution, but have not been
informed of the hand of God in the history of our country,
I have not been educated.

If I can play the piano, the violin, six other instruments, and can write music that moves men
to tears, but have not been taught to listen to the Director of the universe and worship Him,
I have not been educated.

If I can run cross-country races, star in basketball and do 100 push-ups without stopping,
but have never been shown how to bend my spirit to do God's will,
I have not been educated.

If I can identify a Picasso, describe the style of da Vinci, and even paint a portrait that earns an A+,
but have not learned that all harmony and beauty comes from a relationship with God,
I have not been educated.

If I graduate with a perfect 4.0 and am accepted at the best university with a full scholarship,
but have not been guided into a career of God's choosing for me,
I have not been educated.

If I become a good citizen, voting at each election and fighting for what is moral and right,
but have not been told of the sinfulness of man and his hopelessness without Christ,
I have not been educated.

However, if one day I see the world as God sees it, and come to know Him,
Whom to know is life eternal, and glorify God by fulfilling His purpose for me,
then, I have been educated!

Used by permission of Association of Christian Schools International.
From *Christian School Comment*, Vol. 20, No. 9, Colorado Springs, Colorado, 1998,

Appendix

Biblical Principles for Achieving Kingdom Education

Kingdom education is the life-long, Bible-based, Christ-centered process of leading a child into a new identity with Christ and developing him/her according to the specific abilities given to him/ her by Christ so that the child will be empowered to live a life characterized by love, trust, and obedience to Christ.[1]

The ultimate goal of kingdom education is to develop a mature disciple of Jesus Christ whose life glorifies God.

God's Word provides each Christian with principles needed to put kingdom education into practice. These biblical principles must be studied, understood, and practiced in every aspect of life regardless of age. However, it is extremely critical that these principles be carefully and diligently applied to children and youth.

It is common knowledge that the easiest time in life to capture a person's heart for Christ is during the childhood years. The home, church, and school must give full attention to these biblical principles for children and youth from birth through maturity. As you study each principle, give careful attention to the biblical application the principle has to everyday life.

Principle #1: *The education of children and youth is the primary responsibility of parents.*

Lo, children are an heritage of the Lord (Ps. 127:3, KJV).

And thou shalt teach them diligently unto thy children, and shalt talk of them when thou sittest in thine house, and when thou walkest by the way, and when thou liest down, and when thou risest up. And thou shalt bind them for a sign upon thine hand, and they shall be as frontlets between thine eyes. And thou shalt write them upon the posts of thy house, and on thy gates (Deut. 6:7-9, KJV).

And ye shall teach them your children, speaking of them when thou sittest in thine house, and when thou walkest by the way, when thou liest down, and when thou risest up (Deut. 11:19, KJV).

We will not hide them from their children, showing to the generation to come the praises of the Lord, and his strength, and his wonderful works that he hath done. For he established a testimony in Jacob, and appointed a law in Israel, which he commanded our fathers, that they should make them known to their children (Ps. 78:4-5, KJV).

Train up a child in the way he should go: and when he is old, he will not depart from it (Prov. 22:6, KJV).

And did not he make one? Yet had he the residue of the spirit. And wherefore one? That he might seek a godly seed (Mal. 2:15, KJV).

And, ye fathers, provoke not your children to wrath: but bring them up in the nurture and admonition of the Lord (Eph. 6:4, KJV).

These passages make it clear that parents are responsible to God for the education or training of their children. Another way of interpreting Psalm 127:3 is *children are God's homework assignment to parents.* Even if parents delegate some areas of their child's education to others, they are still answerable to God for what and how their children are taught.

Malachi 2 makes it clear that God desires parents to develop godly off-spring. This is an awesome task, and it takes maximum effort on the part of parents to accomplish. As our society becomes more and more secular, we increasingly encounter the false notion that the education of young people is a shared responsibility. Secularists say parents do have certain responsibilities but so do the local, state, and federal governments. At each level of government, various branches are constantly vying to assume more and more of this responsibility.

Application

Christian parents must make sure that they are assuming total responsibility for the education of their children, and to do so, parents must constantly ask themselves certain questions.

1. Who or what is in control of educating my child at home? What training is being done directly by me, the parent? What influence do I allow the media to have on my child at home? Do I know what my child is seeing, hearing or doing while at home?
2. Do I know what my child is being taught in my neighborhood? What are other parents or peers teaching my child when they are together?
3. What is my child being taught in church, Sunday school, and other church related activities?
4. What is my child learning at school? From teachers? From textbooks? From the curriculum? From other students? From the school's policies and procedures?

Parents soon realize that it is a tremendous task to assume direct responsibility in each of these areas. Therefore, it is important that parents follow additional biblical principles as they endeavor to take responsibility for their child's education.

Principle #2: *The education of children and youth is a 24-hours-a-day, 7-days-a-week process that must take place from birth through maturity.*

And thou shalt teach them diligently unto thy children, and shalt talk of them when thou sittest in thine house, and when thou walkest by the way, and when thou liest down, and when thou risest up (Deut. 6:7, KJV).

Ye shall teach them your children, speaking of them when thou sittest in thine house, and when thou walkest by the way, when thou liest down, and when thou risest up (Deut. 11:19, KJV).

Train up a child in the way he should go: and when he is old, he will not depart from it (Prov. 22:6, KJV).

A high percentage of Christian parents have heard and even memorized Proverbs 22:6. We want to claim this as a promise that will assure us that our children will eventually walk with the Lord if we give them some training from a biblical perspective early in life. However, most of us fail to comprehend how intense this training needs to be.

The concept communicated by the phrase *train up a child* is that this is a continual process that starts at birth. *When he is old* tells us that this process does not end until the individual reaches maturity.

God gives us instruction in Deuteronomy 6 when He states that parents must teach their children diligently with intense, highly concentrated, consistent effort. This effort must take place

1. When our children get up each morning;
2. When they are at home and around the house;
3. When they are away from the house; and
4. When they lie down to go to sleep.

The only time we should not be diligently teaching our children the things of God is when they are asleep.

Application
Christian parents need to answer these questions to see if they are following this principle of kingdom education.

1. What am I doing to diligently teach my child the things of God when he awakens each day?
2. How am I diligently teaching my child God's ways while he is at home?
3. Is my child being taught God's truth in all of the activities he is involved in away from home? (Answer as it relates to schooling, recreational activities, and even any work in which the child may be involved.)

4. What am I doing to reinforce God's Word in my child when he finishes each day and goes to bed?

Principle #3: *The education of children and youth must have as its primary goals the salvation and discipleship of the next generation.*

> *Go ye therefore, and teach all nations, baptizing them in the name of the Father, and of the Son, and of the Holy Ghost: Teaching them to observe all things whatsoever I have commanded you: and, lo, I am with you always, even unto the end of the world. Amen (Matt. 28:19-20, KJV).*

> *That the generation to come might know them, even the children which should be born; who should arise and declare them to their children: That they might set their hope in God, and not forget the works of God, but keep his commandments (Ps. 78:6-7, KJV).*

Philip May, in his book *Which Way to Educate?* compares today's educator to the field general who has become so involved in the details and strategies of the immediate battle that he has lost sight of the overall strategy of the war or has actually forgotten why it is being fought.[2] Christian parents must never forget that the only goal with true meaning for why we educate our children is for them to know Jesus Christ as their personal savior.

If our children become National Merit® scholars and do not know Christ, what have we achieved of lasting value? Christ told His disciples that He wanted them to make other disciples, giving them a new identity in Christ and empowering them into a lifelong relationship with Christ characterized by love, trust, and obedience.

As we assume our responsibilities to diligently teach our children God's ways and we do this all day long, we must also strive to see them follow Christ in all they do. In fact, we can know that we have been successful in this task when we see our children and our grandchildren teach their children to know God and keep His commandments.

Application
Christians must develop a single-minded focus on the purpose behind the education of their children. This purpose is to see their children become

mature followers of Christ. As we ask these questions, we can evaluate how well we are doing in practicing this principle.

1. Am I consistently sharing the gospel with my children?
2. Am I a mature disciple of Christ, reflecting a life characterized by love, trust, and obedience to Him?
3. Do all the educational efforts that I provide my child, both at home and away from home, point him to Christ and help him follow Christ? (This must be applied to all a child does, such as music, movies, recreation, schooling, sports, and so on.)

Principle #4: *The education of children and youth must be based on God's Word as absolute truth.*

Heaven and earth shall pass away, but my words shall not pass away (Matt. 24:35, KJV).

Forever, O LORD, thy word is settled in heaven (Ps. 119:89, KJV).

The grass withereth, the flower fadeth: but the word of our God shall stand for ever (Isa. 40:8, KJV).

Man constantly searches for truth. Life has no meaning apart from truth. When Pilate was trying to make sense out of the dilemma he faced concerning Jesus, he asked Jesus, "What is truth?" (John 18:38, KJV). Our society declares truth is determined only by experience. It has been redefined as anything that is "legally accurate." But God's Word is eternal and, therefore, is man's only source of truth. This means that everything man studies must be scrutinized through the lens of Scripture, the only way to find true knowledge that will lead us to wisdom.

When God's Word is removed from any facet of education, that education becomes mere human indoctrination. Such education always evolves into empty philosophies that spoil and deceive because it follows after the traditions of man and the rudiments of the world rather than after Christ. Whatever we teach children and youth must be based on the absolute truth found in God's Word.

Application

As parents evaluate everything that is being taught to their children according to God's Word, these questions will provide a framework for considering present and future actions.

1. Do we, as parents, know God's Word and are we growing in this knowledge by daily study and meditation?
2. Is what we are teaching our children at home, both in words and actions, founded on the truth of God's Word?
3. Do we know what is being taught to our children through the media, entertainment, recreation, church, Sunday school, and school?
4. Is everything that is being taught to our children outside the home grounded in the Word of God? This applies to church, school, and other activities.

Principle #5: *The education of children and youth must hold Christ preeminent in all of life.*

In whom (Jesus) are hid all the treasures of wisdom and knowledge (Col. 2:3, KJV).

Woe unto you, lawyers! for ye have taken away the key of knowledge: ye entered not in yourselves, and them that were entering in ye hindered (Luke 11:52, KJV).

As ye have therefore received Christ Jesus the Lord, so walk ye in him: Rooted and built up in him, and stablished in the faith, as ye have been taught, abounding therein with thanksgiving. Beware lest any man spoil you through philosophy and vain deceit, after the tradition of men, after the rudiments of the world, and not after Christ. For in him dwelleth all the fullness of the Godhead bodily. And ye are complete in him, which is the head of all principality and power (Col. 2:6-10, KJV).

Because of the sacrifice Christ made on the cross on behalf of all men and in humble obedience to His Father, His name has been exalted above all other names. In fact, the Bible states that Jesus not only created everything but everything was created for Him.

Christ is to be preeminent in everything—period. The education of our children and youth must be centered on Christ. By doing this, it will lead us to the goal of seeing our children living in a personal, intimate love relationship with Jesus. Christ must be at the center or heart of all we teach our children.

In the 1600's, John Milton wrote, "The end then of learning is to repair the ruins of our first parents by regaining to know God aright, and out of that knowledge to love him, to imitate him, to be like him."[3]

Application

Have we lost our first love like the church at Ephesus did (Rev. 2:1-7)? The answers to certain questions can help us evaluate whether Christ is preeminent in our lives and in the education of our children and youth.

1. Do our children know that Christ is our first love by our actions concerning
   • how we live at home?
   • our church attendance and involvement?
   • the stewardship of our lives including our time, talent and treasure?
   • how and what we tell them to do?
2. Is Christ the preeminent focus of our church as it relates to training our children? This would include worship, Sunday School, and other activities.
3. Is Christ the center of our children's schooling?
4. Are our family activities such that Christ would be comfortable and welcome?

Principle #6: *The education of children and youth must not hinder the spiritual and moral development of the next generation.*

Whoso shall offend one of these little ones which believe in me, it were better for him that a millstone were hanged about his neck, and that he were drowned in the depth of the sea (Matt. 18:6, KJV).

Then were there brought unto him little children, that he should put his hands on them, and pray: and the disciples rebuked them. But Jesus said, Suffer little children, and forbid them not, to come unto me: for of such is the kingdom of heaven (Matt. 19:13-14, KJV).

They brought young children to him, that he should touch them: and his disciples rebuked those that brought them. But when Jesus saw it, he was much displeased, and said unto them, Suffer the little children to come unto me, and forbid them not: for of such is the kingdom of God. Verily I say unto you, Whosoever shall not receive the kingdom of God as a little child, he shall not enter therein. And he took them up in his arms, put his hands upon them, and blessed them (Mark 10:13-16, KJV).

They brought unto him also infants, that he would touch them: but when his disciples saw it, they rebuked them. But Jesus called them unto him, and said, Suffer little children to come unto me, and forbid them not: for of such is the kingdom of God. Verily I say unto you, Whosoever shall not receive the kingdom of God as a little child shall in no wise enter therein (Luke 18: 15-17, KJV).

Jesus showed a special love for children throughout His earthly ministry. When the disciples tried to keep children from getting too close to Jesus, He rebuked them very firmly. It was in this context that Jesus made statements about the seriousness of offending a young person as noted in the passages above.

Sometimes we think of offending children only in means of physical abuse, but anything that hinders their moral and spiritual development is the epitome of child abuse.

Application

The big question we must answer concerning the education of our children and youth is simply

- Are our children being taught anything that will draw them away from Jesus?

This test must be applied to anything and everything that we are teaching them or allowing others to teach them at home, church, school, or in the community. The question becomes a huge issue when we apply it to who their friends are; what they listen to, see, or read; and what they are being taught in school.

Principle #7: *The education of children and youth, if and when delegated to others by parents, must be done by teachers chosen with utmost care to ensure that they all follow these principles.*

Thou shalt provide out of all the people able men, such as fear God, men of truth, hating covetousness; and place such over them, to be rulers of thousands, and rulers of hundreds, rulers of fifties, and rulers of tens (Ex. 18:21, KJV).

This child I prayed; and the Lord hath given me my petition which I asked of him: Therefore also I have lent him to the LORD; as long as he liveth he shall be lent to the LORD (1 Sam. 1: 27-28, KJV).

The child Samuel ministered unto the LORD before Eli. And the word of the LORD was precious in those days; there was no open vision. And it came to pass at that time, when Eli was laid down in his place, and his eyes began to wax dim, that he could not see; And ere the lamp of God went out in the temple of the LORD, where the ark of God was, and Samuel was laid down to sleep; That the LORD called Samuel: and he answered, Here am I. And he ran unto Eli, and said, Here am I; for thou calledst me. And he said, I called not; lie down again. And he went and lay down. And the LORD called yet again, Samuel. And Samuel arose and went to Eli, and said, Here am I; for thou didst call me. And he answered, I called not, my son; lie down again. Now Samuel did not yet know the LORD, neither was the word of the LORD yet revealed unto him. And the LORD called Samuel again the third time. And he arose and went to Eli, and said, Here am I; for thou didst call me. And Eli perceived that the LORD had called the child. Therefore Eli said unto Samuel, Go, lie down: and it shall be, if he call thee, that thou shalt say, Speak, LORD; for thy servant heareth. So Samuel went and lay down in his place. And the LORD came, and stood, and called as at other times, Samuel, Samuel. Then Samuel answered, Speak; for thy servant heareth (1 Sam. 3:1-10, KJV).

The task of raising children is awesome. It is becoming more demanding with each passing day. Every parent will in some way delegate some of the responsibility in the process of properly educating his/her children. This happens when we take them to church, allow them to go on the Internet, or send them to school.

When Moses was trying to educate the children of Israel to know and follow God, Jethro told him he had better delegate some of the task to others if he planned to survive. However, Jethro warned Moses to be extremely careful to check the character of the person to whom he would delegate any portion of this responsibility. In essence, each person had to fear God, love truth and hate covetousness (Ex. 18:21).

Application

Consider those you allow to help in educating your children. Make a list of every person, institution, organization, and so forth that is teaching your children about any aspect of life. Then ask these questions.

1 Does this person fear God, love truth, and hate covetousness?
2. What can you do to ensure that such people are the only ones that you allow to help you educate your children?

While it is true that we cannot control this in every situation, this principle can and must be applied in the major areas of life where our children are receiving training.

Principle #8: *The education of children and youth results in the formation of lifestyles or worldviews that will be patterned after the belief systems or worldviews of their teachers.*

> *The disciple is not above his master: but every one that is perfect shall be as his master (Luke 6:40, KJV).*

> *Those things, which ye have both learned, and received, and heard, and seen in me, do: and the God of peace shall be with you (Phil. 4:9, KJV).*

Every person has a worldview or an underlying belief system that drives his or her attitudes and actions in life. A person can hold one of two possible worldviews—a God-centered worldview or a man-centered worldview. The individual's worldview is primarily determined by that of his teacher(s).

Everyone who teaches others influences them in three ways: by their content, what they say; by their communication, how they say it; and by their conduct, how they live. No one can teach out of a philosophical vacuum. Their beliefs and values will come out and these will help shape the beliefs and values of those whom they teach.

George Barna claims that only 7-8 percent of today's Christians have a biblical understanding of life.[4] Following this principle would cause us to conclude that today's Christians have been educated by a majority of people (influences) who did not possess a God-centered world view.

Application
Ask yourself the following questions.
1. Do I have a God-centered worldview? Do I think and act from a biblical perspective of life?
2. What type of worldview is my child receiving and seeing in our home, in our church, in his school?
3. What type of worldview is being presented in the music my children listen to? in the media they see and read? in the textbooks they study?

Principle #9: *The education of children and youth must lead to true wisdom by connecting all knowledge to a biblical worldview frame of reference.*

Get wisdom, get understanding: forget it not. … Wisdom is the principle thing; therefore get wisdom: and with all thy getting get understanding (Prov. 4:5,7 KJV).

The fear of the LORD is the beginning of wisdom: and the knowledge of the holy is understanding (Prov. 9:10 KJV).

The heavens declare the glory of God; and the firmament sheweth his handiwork (Ps. 19:1).

The invisible things of him from the creation of the world are clearly seen, being understood by the things that are made, even his eternal power and Godhead; so that they are without excuse (Rom. 1:20).

In whom (Christ) are hid all the treasures of wisdom and knowledge (Col. 2:3, KJV).

Nancy Pearcey in her book *Total Truth* states "We must begin by being utterly convinced that there is a biblical perspective on everything—not just on spiritual matters. … The fear of some "god" is the beginning of every proposed system of knowledge. … God is the sole source of the entire created order. No other gods compete with Him; no natural forces exist on their own; nothing receives its nature or existence from another source. Thus His Word, or laws, or creation ordinances give the world its order and structure. … There is no philosophically or spiritually neutral subject matter."[5]

God created the entire universe—including every fact found in every subject one studies. Scripture makes it clear that God reveals His very character and nature to us through our understanding of His created world. The education that we provide our children must not merely give our children knowledge but must lead to true wisdom and understanding by causing children to see the God-intended meaning found in everything they learn.

If any part of our children's education is presented as if it is spiritually neutral, it results in causing our children to think that God is irrelevant to some aspects of life. This will lead to them dividing their lives into two compartments—the secular and the sacred.

Application

Ask yourself these questions.

1. Do I believe that there is some knowledge that is spiritually neutral?
2. Have I developed a biblical frame of reference (worldview) that causes me to interpret the meaning of all knowledge and every aspect of life with its God-intended meaning?
3. Does the education my children receive at home, church and school require them to submit their minds to God and does it lead them to interpret every aspect of creation in the light of His Word?

Principle #10: *The education of children and youth must have a view of the future that includes the eternal perspective.*

If ye then be risen with Christ, seek those things which are above, where Christ sits on the right hand of God. Set your affection on things above, not on things on the earth (Col. 3:1-2, KJV).

And whatsoever you do, do it heartily, as to the Lord, and not unto men; Knowing that of the Lord ye shall receive the reward of the inheritance: for ye serve the Lord Christ (Col. 3:23-24, KJV).

Lay not up for yourselves treasures upon earth, where moth and rust doth corrupt, and where thieves break through and steal: But lay up for yourselves treasures in heaven, where neither moth nor rust doth corrupt, and where thieves do not break through nor steal: For where your treasure is, there will your heart be also (Matt. 6:19-21, KJV).

These all died in faith, not having received the promises, but having seen them afar off, and were persuaded of them, and embraced them, and confessed that they were strangers and pilgrims on the earth (Heb. 11:13, KJV).

I am now ready to be offered, and the time of my departure is at hand. I have fought a good fight, I have finished my course, I have kept the faith: Henceforth there is laid up for me a crown of righteousness, which the Lord, the righteous judge, shall give me at that day: and not to me only, but unto all them also that love his appearing (2 Tim. 4:6-8, KJV).

None of these things move me, neither count I my life dear unto myself, so that I might finish my course with joy, and the ministry, which I have received of the Lord Jesus, to testify the gospel of the grace of God (Acts 20:24, KJV).

God places a two-fold calling on every child's life. The first and most important call on a child's life is an eternal call. It is God's desire that each child come to know Jesus Christ as his personal Lord and Savior. The second call is a temporal call. This involves God's call for a person to live a life of service to Christ while here on earth.

The education of children and youth must not only prepare them for a life of service here but also to stand before God for eternity. This eternal perspective must be part of the entire educational process. It is very natural to focus only on this temporal life when it comes to education. But if this is the only focus of education, then individual success will be measured in temporal financial achievement. Financial success is the dominant goal of secular education today.

Application
Ask yourself these questions.
1. Why do I want my child to have a good education?
2. How does my life reflect an eternal perspective as I live it before my children?
3. How is the eternal perspective seen in the teaching of my children that takes place in my home, the church, and the school?
4. Do I want my children to get a good job and have a comfortable lifestyle more than I want God to use them in any way He sees fit?

Summary
The education of our children and youth is an awesome responsibility that every Christian parent must be willing to assume. Remember that children are God's homework assignment to parents. Psalm 127:5 states that when a parent has successfully completed his homework assignment, "they shall not be ashamed, but they shall speak with the enemies in the gate."

Oswald Chambers commented on this verse:

> Have I been able to reproduce my own kind spiritually? If so, in a time of difficulty I will be brought through magnificently victorious; but woe be to the spiritual man who has never produced his own kind, when the difficulties come there is none to assist, he is isolated and lonely.[6]

Many Christian parents are becoming increasingly concerned about their children's education with each passing day. The violence that is growing in society, especially in our youth, is causing great alarm. Too often, the first and sometimes only question that parents ask is Where should I send my child to school? Should they go to Christian, home, private, or public schools?

Too often this question leads to heated debates. Since God's Word does not address the Where? question directly, any position can be justified and rationalized. At the same time, the next generation continues in a moral tailspin, seemingly out of control. In too many cases, where they are attending school doesn't seem to make a difference. This is because Christian parents are not following biblical principles when it comes to the education of their children and youth.

The debate must never be about where should Christians send their children to school. The debate needs to be about how does God want Christians to educate their children? It is not about Christian versus public schools. It is about biblical education versus secular education. I hope you have given careful attention to the 10 biblical principles relating to the education of children and youth. All 10 principles must be followed fully if we are going to fulfill the definition of kingdom education.

There are an estimated 20-25 million children and youth from church families. This huge number represents a tremendous potential for a powerful spiritual army if they are educated and enter into adult life knowing God and thinking and acting from a biblical worldview. If we earnestly apply these principles to the education of our children, the *where* question will be more accurately answered and the potential to capture the next generation and their world for Christ can become a reality.

NOTES

FOREWORD
1. Josh McDowell and Bob Hostetler, *Beyond Belief to Convictions* (Wheaton, Ill.: Tyndale House Publishers, 2002), 298.

INTRODUCTION: THE IMPORTANCE OF EDUCATION
1. George Barna, quoted from a seminar presentation "What Effective Churches Have Discovered," Baton Rouge, La., April 1997.
2. Ravi Zacharias, "Evangelistic Preaching in the 21st Century: Barriers of the Mind and Hungers of the Heart." Address to the Amsterdam 2000 conference sponsored by the Billy Graham Evangelistic Association, July 29–August 6, 2000 in The Netherlands, <http//www.amsterdam2000.org/s_zacharias.asp> (6 August 2002).
3. George Barna, "Americans Are Most Likely to Base Truth on Feelings," *Barna Research Online,* 12 February 2002, <http://www.barna.org/cgi-bin/PagePressRelease.asp?PressReleaseID=106&Reference=B> (10 September 2002).
4. Frank Gaebelein, *Christian Education in a Democracy* (Colorado Springs: Association of Christian Schools International, 1995), 11-12.
5. Christian Overman, *Assumptions that Affect Our Lives* (Chatsworth, Calif.: Micah 6:8, 1996), 22.

CHAPTER 1: IN THE BEGINNING
1. John Milton, "Of Education," in *Basic Writings In Christian Education,* ed. Kendig Brubaker Culley (Philadelphia: The Westminister Press, 1960), 24.
2. *Webster's New World Dictionary of the American Language,* college ed., s.v. "education."
3. "The Way We Live Now Poll," *New York Times Magazine*, Sunday, 7 May 2000, sec. 6, p. 58.

CHAPTER 2: DEFINING KINGDOM EDUCATION
1. Glen Schultz, *A Parent's Greatest Joy* (Nashville: Convention Press, 1997), 15.
2. Gene Mims, *Thine Is the Kingdom* (Nashville: LifeWay Press, 1997), 18.
3. Henry T. Blackaby and Claude V. King, *Experiencing God: Knowing and Doing the Will of God* (Nashville: LifeWay Press, 1990).

4. W. A. Harper, *Character Building in Colleges* (New York: The Abingdon Press, 1928), 13-14.

5. Author unknown.

6. Simon, Howe, Kirschenbaum, *Values Clarification: A Handbook of Practical Strategies for Teachers and Students* (New York: Hart Publishing Co., 1972), back cover, quoted in Josh McDowell, *Knowing Good from Evil* (2002), <http://www.Josh.org> (1 November 2002).

7. Timothy D. Crater, "The Unproclaimed Priests of Public Education," *Christianity Today*, 10 April 1981, 46, quoted in Russ Wise, "Education and New Age Humanism," <http://www.probe.org/docs/newageed.html> (8 October 2002), "Relativism is the Key."

8. Ibid., 47.

9. Helen M. Hughes, *Inquiries in Sociology* (Newton, Mass.: Allyn and Bacon, 1972), page 37, quoted in Russ Wise, "Education and New Age Humanism," <http://www.probe.org/docs/newageed.html> (8 October 2002), "The Great Brain Robbery."

10. Richard Rorty, *Contingency, Irony, and Solidarity* (New York: Cambridge University Press, 1989), 5, quoted in "Multiculturalism," <http://www.probe.org/docs/multicul.html> (8 October 2002), "What is Multiculturalism?"

11. Josephson Institute of Ethics, "Making Ethical Decisions: What is Ethics Anyway?" June 2001, <http://www.josephsoninstitute.org/MED/MED-what is ethics.htm> (14 May 2002)

12. Os Guinness, *Fit Bodies Fat Minds* (Grand Rapids, MI: Baker Books, 1994), 38.

13. Paul Kienel, Ollie Gibbs, and Sharon Berry, eds. *Philosophy of Christian School Education* (Colorado Springs, CO: Association of Christian Schools International, 1995), 148.

14. Paul A. Kienel, "Let's Preserve the Family," *Christian School Comment, Vol. 11, No. 8* (Colorado Springs, CO: Association of Christian Schools International).

15. Charles Swindoll, *Growing Deep in the Christian Life* (Portland, Ore.: Multnomah Press, 1986), 56.

16. Woodrow M. Kroll, *The Vanishing Ministry* (Grand Rapids: Kreger Publications, 1991).

17. Oswald Chambers, *The Complete Works of Oswald Chambers*, (Grand Rapids: Discovery House Publishers, 2000), 265.

18. Dr. Albert Mohler, Addressing Christian educators at the ACSI Teachers Convention, Columbus, Ohio, October 2001.

19. Philip May, *Which Way to Educate?* (Chicago: Moody Press, 1972), 26-27.

CHAPTER 3: THE END RESULT OF EDUCATION

1. Charles Colson, *The Body: Being Light in Darkness* (Dallas: Word Publishing, 1992), 186.

2. John Blanchard, "Can We Live with Public Education?" *Moody Monthly* (October 1971): 88-89.

3. Milton, *"Of Education,"* 192-204.

4. May, *Which Way to Educate?* 60-61.

5. Kienel, Gibbs, and Berry, eds. *Philosophy of Christian School Education,* 7.

6. E. Ray Moore, Jr., *Let My Children Go* (Columbia, S.C.: Gilead Media, 2002), 11.

7. Patrick M. Morley, *The Rest of Your Life: A Road Map for Christians Who Want a Deeper Understanding of What to Believe and How to Live It* (Grand Rapids, Mich.: ZondervanPublishingHouse, 1998), 106.

8. Study note on Daniel 1:7 in *The Believer's Study Bible, New King James Version,* W.A. Criswell, ed. (Nashville: Thomas Nelson Publishers, 1991), 1178.

9. Charles Colson, "Passing the Torch to Future Generations: Lessons from a Dictator," *BreakPoint Online,* no. 011123, 23 November 2001, <http://www.breakpoint.org/Breakpoint/ChannelRoot/WelcomeGroup/AboutBreakPoint/> (1 November 2002).

10. Morley, *The Rest of Your Life,* 106.

11. David A. Noebel, *Understanding the Times: the Religious Wordviews of Our Day and the Search for Truth* (Eugene, Ore.: Harvest House Publishers, 1994).

12. Colson, *The Body: Being Light in Darkness,* 186.

13. Ibid., 189.

14. Tim LaHaye, *The Battle for the Mind* (Old Tappan, NJ: Fleming H. Revell Co., 1980), 71.

15. LaHaye, *The Battle for the Mind,* 70.

16. Ibid., 68.

17. George Barna, *What Americans Believe: An Annual Survey of Values and Religious Views in the United States* (Ventura, Calif.: Regal, 1991), 85, as quoted in Charles Colson, *The Body: Being Light in Darkness,* 178.

18. George Barna, "How America's Faith Has Changed Since 9-11," *Barna Research Online,* 26 November 2001, <http://www.barna.org/cgi-bin/PagePressRelease.asp?PressReleaseID=102Reference=A> (27 November 2001).

19. LaHaye, *The Battle for the Mind,* 60.

20. Alvin Toffler, "The Psychology of the Future," *Readings in the Socio-Cultural Foundations of Education,* Burbach, Hackett, McMahon, and Wagoner, eds. (Sarasota, Fla.: Omni Press, 1974), 126.

21. Gerald Stiles, Professor, History of American Education, from a lecture given at a South Carolina Christian school administrators meeting sponsored by the Association of Christian Schools International (Charleston, S.C.: 1995).

22. Colson, *The Body: Being Light in Darkness*, 152.

23. Ibid., 154.

24. Ibid., 156.

25. Gaebelein, *Christian Education in a Democracy*, 18.

26. Morley, *The Rest of Your Life*, 97.

27. Ibid., 3.

28. Ibid., 96.

29. McDowell and Hostetler, *Beyond Belief to Convictions*, 5.

30. Morley, *The Rest of Your Life*, 87.

CHAPTER 4: THE INFLUENCES OF A TEACHER

1. Frank Gaebelein, *The Pattern of God's Truth* (Chicago: Moody Press, 1968), 37.

2. Albert Mohler, "Christian Education, Minus Scripture, a 'Lie'" *Baptist Messenger* (Oklahoma City: Dec. 4, 1997), 11.

3. Morley, *The Rest of Your Life*, 95.

4. Ibid., 94.

CHAPTER 5: GOD'S ASSIGNMENT FOR PARENTS

1. Schultz, *A Parent's Greatest Joy*, 1.

2. George Barna, "Born Again Adults Less Likely to Co-Habit, Just as Likely to Divorce," *Barna Research Online*, 6 August 2001, <http://www.barna.org/cgi-bin/PagePressRelease.asp?PressReleaseID=95&Reference=C> (14 October 2002).

3. John MacArthur, *What the Bible Says About Parenting* (Nashville: Word Publishing, 2000), xi.

4. Ibid., 12.

5. Overman, *Assumptions That Affect Our Lives*, 121.

6. MacArthur, *What the Bible Says About Parenting*, 19.

7. Bruce Wilkinson, *First Hand Faith* (Sisters, Ore.: Multnomah Books, 1996), 37.

8. Larry Burkett, *Financial Parenting* (Colorado Springs: Chariot Victor Publishing, Cook Communications, 1996), 39.

9. Francis Curran, *The Churches and Schools: American Protestantism and Popular Elementary Education* (Chicago: Loyola University Press, 1954), Preface.

10. Overman, *Assumptions That Affect Our Lives*, 122.

11. MacArthur, *What the Bible Says About Parenting*, 71.

12. Ibid., 71.

13. Burkett, *Financial Parenting*, 43.

14. Wilkinson, *First Hand Faith*, 38.

15. Ibid., 40.

16. These are excerpts from the testimony of Lorin Bourguein given on August 7, 2001, in Beaumont, Texas. Reprinted with permission.

CHAPTER 6: THE TRAINING PROCESS

1. Overman, *Assumptions That Affect Our Lives*, 137.

CHAPTER 7: FINDING HELP

1. Schultz, *A Parent's Greatest Joy*, 15.

2. MacArthur, *What the Bible Says About Parenting*, 19, 21.

3. Charles Swindoll, *Stress Fractures* (Portland, Ore.: Multnomah Press, 1990), 24-26.

CHAPTER 8: THE IMPORTANCE OF THE CHURCH

1. Mims, *Thine Is the Kingdom*, 99.

2. Ibid., 18.

3. Burkett, *Financial Parenting*.

4. Ibid., 43

CHAPTER 9: THE GREAT COMMISSION

1. Mims, *Thine Is the Kingdom*, 101.

CHAPTER 10: SUPPORTING THE HOME

1. Billie Friel, Pastor, First Baptist Church, Mt Juliet, Tennessee, from a sermon on the home, 1997.

2. Art Toalston, "In Defense of the Family," *SBC Life* (April 2001), <http://www.sbclife.net/articles/2001/04/sla1.asp> (11 September 2002).

3. John MacArthur, *What the Bible Says About Parenting*, ix.

4. Gaebelein, *Christian Education in a Democracy*, 8.

5. George Barna, "Churches Have Opportunity to Help Parents," *Barna Research Online*, 15 January 1998, <http://www.barna.org/cgi-bin/PagePressRelease.asp?PressReleaseID=19Reference=C> (8 May 2001).

6. Gaebelein, *Christian Education in a Democracy*, 10.

7. Wilkinson, *First Hand Faith*, 235.

8. Jay Strack, quoted in Victor Lee and Jerry Pipes, *Family to Family: Families Making a Difference* (Alpharetta, GA: North American Mission Board, Southern Baptist Convention, 1999), 50 and 124.

9. Wilkinson, *First Hand Faith*, 174.

10. Warren A. Nord, *Religion & American Education: Rethinking a National Dilemma* (Chapel Hill, N.C.: University of North Carolina Press, 1995), 61.

CHAPTER 11: THE SCHOOL AND THE HOME

1. James Carper, "The Christian Day School," Carper, Hunt, eds., *Religious Schooling in America* (Birmingham, Ala.: Religious Education Press, 1984), 118.

2. R. Michaelsen, *Piety in the Public School* (New York: The Macmillan Company, 1970), 51.

3. "The General Laws and Liberties of New Plymouth Colony," revised and published in June, 1971 in W. Brigham (Ed.), *The Compact with the Charter and Laws of the Colony of new Plymouth* (Boston: Dutton and Wentworth, Printers to the State).

4. Glen Schultz, *A Study of the Religious Beliefs and Practices of Christian School Graduates* (Charlottesville, Va.: University of Virginia, 1994), 38.

5. May, *Which Way to Educate?* 101.

6. Blanchard, "Can We Live with Public Education?" 88-89.

7. P. Hirst, "Public and Private Values and Religious Educational Content," in Theodore R. Sizer, ed., *Religion and Public Education* (Boston: Houghton Mifflin, 1967), 329-339.

8. H. Shelton Smith, *Faith and Nurture* (New York: Charles Scribner's Sons, 1941), 202.

9. James C. Dobson and Gary L. Bauer, *Children at Risk: The Battle for the Hearts and Minds of Our Kids* (Dallas: Word Publishing, 1990), 19-20.

10. Ibid., 35.

11. Ibid., 37.

12. Linda Seebach, "Let's Restore Separation of Church and State," (Commentary) *Gazette Telegraph*, January 18, 1995.

13. C. F. Potter, *Humanism: A New Religion* (1930) in D. L. Cuddy "Are Secular Humanists Seeking Our Children's Minds? You Bet," *Commercial Appeal,* August 5, 1986, Memphis, Tenn.

14. Paul Blanshard, *The Humanist* (March-April, 1976) in D. L. Cuddy "Are Secular Humanists Seeking Our Children's Minds? You Bet," *Commercial Appeal,* 5 August 1986 (Memphis, Tenn.).

15. John Goodland, "Schooling for the Future" in Roland M. Travis, "Should the Children of God Be Educated in the Temple of Baal?" *Presbyterian Journal*, 13 February 1985, (Asheville, N.C.: God's World Publications, 1985).

16. John Dunphy, "A Religion for a New Age," *The Humanist* 43, no. 1, (January/February 1983): 26.

17. Roger LeRoy Miller, *Economics Today and Tomorrow*, Chapter 17, "Government Spends, Collects and Owes," (New York: Glencoe Division of MacMillian/McGraw-Hill, 1991), 415, quoted in Josh McDowell, *Knowing Good from Evil*.

18. Herbert Sorenson, Marguerite Malm, Garlie A. Forehand, *Psychology for Living, 3rd ed.,* New York: Webster/McGraw-Hill, 1971), 189-190.

19. Morton Botel and John Dawkins, *Communicating,* Grade 2, (Lexington, Mass.: D.C. Heath, 1973), quoted in Josh McDowell, *Knowing Good from Evil*.

20. Beverly J. Armento et. al., "Understanding Pluralism," *A More Perfect Union* (Boston: Houghton Mifflin Company, 1991), 50.

21. Sorenson, Malm, and Forehand, *Psychology for Living,* 319.

22. James A. Banks et al., *World: Adventures in Time and Place* (New York: McGraw-Hill School Division, 2000), 16.

23. Mounir A. Farah, Andrea Berens Karls, *World History: The Human Experience (*New York: Glencoe/McGraw-Hill, 1999), 179, quoted in Josh McDowell, *Knowing Good from Evil*.

24. Robert Hatcher et al., *The Quest for Excellence (*Decatur, Ga.: Bridging the Gap Communications, Inc., 1993), 3, 66.

25. May, *Which Way to Educate?* 24.

26. Ibid., 26-27

CHAPTER 12: THE SCHOOL AND THE CHURCH

1. Curran, *The Churches and Schools,* 5.

2. Schultz, *A Study of the Religious Beliefs and Practices of Christian School Graduates.*

3. Paul Young, "The Marriage of the Church and the Christian School: Why Do They Struggle," *Christian School Education* 1, no. 2 (1997-98): 5-8.

4. Derek J. Keenan, "A Crucial Relationship," *Christian School Education* 1, no. 2 (1997-98): 4.

CHAPTER 13: THE SCHOOL AND THE BIBLE

1. John Morison, *Counsels to Young Men on Modern Infidelity and the Evidences of Christianity* (New York: American Tract Society).

2. Mohler, *Baptist Messenger,* 11.

3. John Piper, "Darwinism on My Front Porch," in *A Godward Life: Book Two: Savoring the Sustenance of God in All of Life* (Sisters, Ore.: Multnomah Publishers, 1999), 158.

4. Gaebelein, *Christian Education in a Democracy,* 1.

5. Benjamin Rush, *Essays, Literary, Moral and Philosophical* (Philadelphia: Thomas and William Bradford, 1806), 113.

6. Benjamin Rush, *The Bible in Schools* (Garland, Tex.: The American Tract Society, 1995), quoted in "The Great Worth of the Bible in School," *Christian School Comment, Vol. 26, No. 8* (Colorado Springs: Association of Christian Schools International, 1995).

7. Rush, *The Bible in Schools.*

8. Fisher Ames, *Notices of the Life and Character of Fisher Ames* (Boston: T. B. Wait and Company, 1809), 134-135.

9. Noah Webster, "On the Education of Youth in America." Reprinted in Frederick Rudolph (Ed.) *Essays on Education in the Early Republic* (Cambridge, Mass.: Harvard Press, 1790), 50-51.

10. Frank Spina, "What Makes It Christian" *Moody Monthly* (Chicago: Moody Press, March 1993): 43.

11. Albert E. Greene, *Reclaiming the Future of Christian Education: A Transforming Vision* (Colorado Springs: Association of Christian Schools International, 1998), 44-45, 100.

12. Greene, *Reclaiming the Future of Christian Education,* 32, 37.

CHAPTER 14: THE DANGER OF DUALISM

1. Blackaby and King, *Experiencing God: Knowing and Doing the Will of God,* 53.

2. Albert Greene, *Thinking Christianly New Patterns for New People* (Medina, Wash.: Alta Vista College Press, 1990), 52-62.

3. Morley, *The Rest of Your Life,* 51.

4. Ibid., 56.

5. Blanchard, "Can We Live with Public Education?" 88-89.

6. Walter Ediger, *The Quest for Excellence in Christian School Education* (Siloam Springs, Ark.: RPA Associates, 1993), 20.

7. Greene, *Reclaiming the Future of Christian Education,* 36.

8. Ediger, *The Quest for Excellence,* 18.

9. Ibid., 18.

10. Blackaby and King, *Experiencing God: Knowing and Doing the Will of God,* 44.

11. Colson, *The Body: Being Light in Darkness,* 187.

12. Greene, *Reclaiming the Future of Christian Education,* 110.

CHAPTER 15: RENEWING THE MIND

1. Harry Blarmires, *The Christian Mind: How Should a Christian Think?* (Ann Arbor, Mich.: Servant Books, 1978), 3.

2. Blarmires, *The Christian Mind,* 67.

3. Os Guinness, *Fit Bodies, Fat Minds,* 14.

4. Morley, *The Rest of Your Life,* 2.

5. Barna, 'What Effective Churches Have Discovered."

6. Guinness, *Fit Bodies Fat Minds,* 136.

7. Charles Swindoll, *Living Above the Level of Mediocrity* (Waco, Tex.: Word Books, 1987), 23-26.

8. Morley, *The Rest of Your Life,* 28.

CHAPTER 16: A CALL TO ACTION

1. May, *Which Way to Educate?* 9.

2. Nord, *Religion & American Education,* 61.

3. Herschel H. Hobbs, *The Baptist Faith and Message* (Nashville: Convention Press, 1971, rev. 1996), 97.

4. Hobbs, *The Baptist Faith and Message,* 97.

5. *The Baptist Faith and Message,* A Statement Adopted by the Southern Baptist Convention, 14 June 2000 (Nashville: LifeWay Christian Resources, 2000).

6. Blackaby and King, *Experiencing God: Knowing and Doing the Will of God,* 87.

EPILOGUE:

1. *The Believer's Study Bible, New King James Version,* 1178.

2. Charles Colson, "Passing the Torch to Future Generations."3. Greene, *Reclaiming the Future of Christian Education,* 29.

4. Bourguein, Testimony.

5. John Piper, "Should Christian Colleges Indoctrinate?" in *A Godward Life, Book Two,* 115-116.

6. Quoted in a sermon by Dr. Glenn Weekley, First Baptist Church, Hendersonville, Tenn., 3 February 2002.

APPENDIX:

1. Glen Schultz, Definition of kingdom education.

2. May, *Which Way to Educate?* 9.

3. Milton, *"Of Education,"* 192-204.

4. George Barna, quoted from a seminar presentation "What Effective Churches Have Discovered," Baton Rouge, Louisiana, April 1997.

5. Nancy Pearcey, *Total Truth: Liberating Christianity from It Cultural Captivity* (Wheaton, IL: Crossway Books, 2004), 44-45.

6. Chambers, *The Complete Works of Oswald Chambers,* 537.

ABOUT THIS BOOK

Dr. Glen Schultz is one of the foremost spokesmen for Christian School education in the world today. He has served God as the administrator of Lynchburg Christian Academy, one of America's finest schools, and as the Southeast Regional Director of the Association of Christian Schools International—the largest group of Evangelical schools in the world.

Glen's remarkable gifts of communication in both speech and in writing have afforded him amazing opportunities to share his vision for Kingdom Education.

Dr. Paul A. Kienel, Founder
Association of Christian Schools International

Glen Schultz hits the nail squarely on the head! With keen insight, years of personal experience and a heart of conviction, Glen challenges Christian parents and leaders alike to recognize the sweeping changes in education over the past several decades. Nothing less than spiritual warfare can reverse the tide of total secularization of education and society. Every parent, every pastor and every educator must link arms to educate our children according to Kingdom principles. The very future of our society is at stake.

James T. Draper, Jr., President Emeritus
LifeWay Christian Resources

There is not a more knowledgeable expert in the field of Christian education than Glen Schultz. The proof is in the pudding, as his family turned out to be a paragon of grace and virtue. Any Christian, and especially any Christian parent, would be doing themselves a tremendous favor by devouring this book. It is rich with the insight and wisdom of a modern-day Solomon.

Dr. James Merritt, Senior Pastor
Cross Pointe Church, Duluth, GA